The
Therapist

Deborah Lewis

The Therapist

Copyright © by Author: Deborah Lewis, June 2020
Edited by Georgina Hatch
Typeset by TamaRe House Publishers
Cover Illustration by Abbastanza Collective Shadun Layne

ISBN: 978-1-908552-77-8

The

Therapist

Acknowledgements

I like to thank my children for their continuous support while writing this book. Carla, Kimberly, Khameera, Sahleem and Sahlee; you are all an inspiration to me.

I also like to thank my friend Roberto who continuously encouraged me to finish this book.

Thanks to Abbastanza Collective Shadun Layne for your creativity and being able to understand my ideas and illustrating cover the artwork.

A great thank you to Paul Simons who supported me, and helped me to put this book together.

Chapter 1

S andy went outside, she saw Michael leaning against her car. She stood still, frozen on the spot, her eyes opened wide, not knowing what to say. She had just told him that she was not at home when he rang her. He stood still, his eyes fixed on hers; saying nothing, but his eyes said a lot. Sandy tried to think of what to say. 'Think, Sandy, think.' She felt his stare penetrating her mind. 'I can't lie, he will know,' she said to herself. Sandy has no problem with a penetrative stare of love and passion, especially during sex, but this stare was different. It said, 'Why did you lie?' She composed herself and greeted him, 'Hi Ras, surprised to see you here, I thought that you would be at work at this time.'

Sandy has been seeing Michael, aka Ras, on and off for about two years. Michael is Jamaican, tall, and with a dark complexion and long flowing locks down his back. He is of medium build with rugged features. His forehead creases display years of stress and worry and, he's always broke. He's not the greatest of lookers but he has charisma and is a good dresser; best of all, he's great in bed. Without this last attribute, Sandy would not have bothered with him. Sandy, on the other hand, is medium height with a caramel complexion and short-cropped hair; she has big cat-shaped eyes and straight features. She is always complimented on her looks. Sandy likes to wear tight-fitted clothes, they accentuate her curves. Her preference is that she loves quality over the name brand, except when it comes to her handbags and shoes. She looks younger than her age and has maintained her shape very well.

Sandy is a mother of 5; twin girls age 21, two boys, one 19 and one 25, and her eldest is a girl aged 28. Sandy calls them her five adults because they are all over 18. She was born in London; her mother and father having come to England from Jamaica at a very young age. She is the eldest of a family of three children, she has one sister and one brother.

'I knew you were lying to me,' said Michael in an angry tone.

'Oh Ras, don't start on me about lying, you're the master of lies,' replied Sandy with a slight smirk.

'What have I lied about now? You're always calling me a liar; do you know what I've been through?'

'How would I know what you've been through when I don't see you and I don't hear from you?'

'What's your problem, Sandy? Is it because I did not meet you at Silvarna's the other night?'

'Oh,' she said, staring at Michael, "So you remembered that you were supposed to meet me? I thought you forgot, I even rang your phone, but it went to voicemail as usual.'

'My battery died,' protested Michael 'You always give me such a hard time, you don't even know what happened'.

Sandy walked up to Michael and looked up at him with her eyes gleaming. Michael looked down at Sandy with his lips close to hers. 'You know you miss me, and you want me, Sandy. So why are you playing games?' he said in a soft caressing voice. Sandy's lips gently brushed against his. She eased her head back and looked into his eyes.

'Ras,' in a calm, low voice, 'you're so full of shit!' She paused. 'Now get the fuck away from my car, I have things to do, and I have no time for your stories! As I keep saying Ras, when I want to hear a story, I will read a book!'

Michael stepped aside and looked at Sandy. She could see the creases forming in his forehead as he looked at her, his eyes turning red. Sandy sat in her car and drove off, tooting her horn as she sped away in her metallic brown Kia Sportage.

Sandy is a qualified therapist; she loves her job but what she loves even more is that she is self-employed. She's a no-nonsense person in work and life. But when it came to relationships; she seems to continuously pick the wrong men. Sandy cared deeply for Michael, although she would never let him know. She liked to keep her feelings close to her chest until she felt safe to open up. There was no security with Ras.

'Caroline, are you home?' asked Sandy,

'Yes, just stepped in from work, where are you?'

'I'm about five minutes from your house, I need someone to talk to,' she said in a wearily tone.

'You sound pissed-off; don't worry I have a glass of rosé waiting for you.'

Sandy and Caroline have been good friends for about five years. Caroline is slim, medium height, with short brown curly hair. She has a round face, small nose, dimples, which are a lot more noticeable when she smiles, and big brown eyes. She also has twins but are 18-year-old boys and a daughter aged 16. Caroline and Sandy come from two separate paths but respect each other's beliefs. Caroline being Christian and therefore believes in God and Jesus. On the other hand, Sandy believes in a higher source and the universe. But what makes their friendship work is that they both agreed to disagree and get on with their friendship. Sandy parked outside Caroline's house. Door number 52. Sandy's door number is 25- she felt that fate had led them to become good friends. She pressed the buzzer.

'Who is it?' asked Caroline in a high-pitched voice.

'Open the door, Caroline; I need a drink,' said Sandy, feeling quite annoyed.

Caroline has a chirpy, fun personality that Sandy really likes but today she was not in the mood for it, she just wanted to sit down with a glass of wine and talk.

Caroline lives in a cul-de-sac and her house has a small front garden and her own driveway, where she parks her black Mercedes Benz. She has a modern three-bedroom, two-storey house; she loves wood and has Parquet flooring right through her passage upstairs and downstairs and oak wood in all the bedrooms and her lounge. She has beige carpet along her stairway which blends with her cream walls. Her kitchen is spacious which enables her to cook and dine in the same room. Caroline loves to entertain which is why she has a double cooker and oven, a large American-style fridge and freezer, and a large pinewood table and chairs which seat 10 people although only four people live in her house. She loves lavish furnishings which she can afford, she's a qualified accountant who works with a few prestige top firms.

Contrary to her home which has warm, earthy colours, Caroline is a very colourful dresser; she has wigs to match every outfit.

'Sandy, you need to stop letting that man get to you,' Caroline attempted to comfort her. 'I thought that you were going shopping.'

Sandy sighed and sat down in Caroline's lounge on her comfy brown leather sofa, then took a sip of her wine.

'I was,' she said, interrupting Caroline, 'but when I stepped out, Ras was standing there leaning on my car.'

'Sandy, it's not for me to give you advice.'

'But you will anyway,' grinned Sandy.

'You're the one who came to my house, and you know how I am, I'm going to say it as it is, just like you do when it's me. This man is forever lying to you and standing you up, you know that he has other women so why do you put up with his crap?'

'I know, babes.'

'I mean,' continued Caroline, 'is his dick that good? There is more dick out there.'

'Yes, it is that good Caroline, he's the first man to make me pulsate and have multiple orgasms. He is truly a pussy specialist I tell you that, but I get your point.'

Sandy closed her eyes and laughed; Caroline looked at her and rolled her eyes.

'What about that other guy you met, what's his name again?' Caroline asked, with a confused look on her face. 'Was it Tinchy or Tic? I don't remember, you and these nicknames, you know I hate nicknames.'

Sandy laughed. 'No, it's Teddy.'

'So why do you call him Teddy?'

'To be honest with you, Caroline, I don't know. He used to be fit and toned; you know the six-pack thing and all that. As he has gotten older, he's a little loose but he was called Teddy before he put the weight on.'

'So, what's his real name, and how old is he?'

'His name is Anthony and he's 53,' answered Sandy.

'That's a bit old for you; I'm surprised you went past the forties.'

'I know, that's true, it's only because I have known him for so long that he gets away with it,' she replied.

'I need to remind you, Sandy, that we plan to find a suitable man for marriage. We decided to do this when we went out for a drink on my birthday last year December. It sounded extreme back then but as time has gone on, we could not of came up with a better pact; so, don't let the team down Sandy. You, Joan and I gave ourselves a year, we have seven months left! You know that Michael is unsuitable as hell, so I'm just saying stop wasting time with dead-beats. We are in our forties, nearing 50. You're closer to 50 than I am, Sandy, so stop with the nicknamed guys.'

Sandy took another sip of her wine and thought about what Caroline had said; but her thought process was distracted by the ringing of her phone.

'This is the third time your phone has rung since you sat down in the space of half an hour. Is it Michael?' asked Caroline.

'No, it's Teddy.'

'So, why don't you answer your phone?'

'Caroline, this man frightens me. Two days ago, I went to Silvarna wine bar to meet Ras but, as you know, he stood me up. Anyway, Teddy was there, he started telling me how he had liked me for a long time, and he would like to take me out for a drink. I thought, well, I don't mind going out for a drink, so I gave him my number, but Caroline, he calls me about 10 times a day.'

'So, you have Michael who never calls you unless he wants something, then Teddy who calls non-stop; these men go from one extreme to the next. What does he talk to you about?' she asked smirking.

'Nothing much, just that he's been thinking of me, and he can't get me off his mind, or he just wants to hear my voice.'

'That's nice, a man paying you attention, there's nothing to be frightened about. What, are you not used to a man giving you so much attention?'

'No, it's not that Caroline; this is just a lot too quickly; it makes me wonder if he has another agenda.'

'Only time will tell Sandy, so what does he look like?'

'Well, he's about 5 foot 11. Medium built, about my complexion. Very short black hair with flecks of grey, small eyes, and straight nose. His beard and moustache are neatly shaven. When he smiles, his eyes quint shut, plus he's a really good dresser, everything matches,' said Sandy with a faraway look in her eyes.

'He sounds nice, better looking than Michael.'

'Enough about me. How is your old man, Patrick?'

'Mean as usual,' she said with a grim look.

Caroline preferred older men. Patrick was 20 years her senior. She believed that older men were a lot more stable and that it was a man's duty to look after his woman. They've been in a 10-year relationship. Patrick owns a construction company alongside his son.

'I take it that he still has not given you the money for you and the children to go to Canada.'

'No, he has not, and he can more than afford to pay for it! I honestly dislike mean men.'

'But you can afford to pay for your holiday yourself.'

'That's why you keep attracting broke men,' responded Caroline with a hint of vexation in her voice. 'I keep telling you,' she went on, 'you need to spend their money and not your own, otherwise they will want to spend yours!'

'Ouch!' said Sandy, with a grin. 'I get your point. Maybe I need to take a few notes out of your book. But I have to love you and leave you. I need to get something in for dinner and call Teddy back.'

'Remember it's our monthly girl's night next week, or should I call it our progress report? I suppose I have to remind Joan as well, she has a bad memory,' said Caroline.

'I know, it's in my diary,' Sandy replied.

Sandy hugged Caroline goodbye and went to her car. As she sat in her car, she heard her phone ringing.

'Hi Teddy,' Sandy replied softly.

'Hi Teddy' he mimicked, 'really Sandy.' Where have you been? Do you know how long I've been ringing your phone?' he said, sounding quite vexed.

'I'm sorry, babes, I was with a client, and I could not answer my phone. Are you okay?'

'Yes, yes babes I'm good, I'm good, I just miss you and I want to see you later, meet me later.'

'Okay, is 8 alright?' she asked.

'8, what time is it now?'

'It's 4.30,' replied Sandy.

'Yeh, 8 is good, it's good.'

'Where should I pick you up?'

'At the pub on Penine Street, babes.'

'Okay, later,' Sandy ended the call.

Sandy chuckled when she hung up the phone; she found it funny that Teddy repeats things two or three times when he speaks. As Sandy drove, she thought about what Caroline had said to her regarding her choice of men; she hoped that Teddy would be different. Sandy is a very private person; she does not like to date men that she already knew, and everyone knew Teddy. She was putting a lot of trust in him about his feelings towards her and hoped that he was sincere. She decided that she would take it slow and not expose their relationship until she felt assured that he was genuine.

Sandy went to Tesco's and brought lamb chops for her adults and salmon for herself, as she did not eat meat. Then went home to cook and get ready to meet Teddy.

Sandy's home is a three-storey, five-bedroom house with a driveway large enough to hold two cars. There is oak wood along her passage floor and carpet in all her bedrooms, lounge, and along her stairway. Sandy loves carpet; she feels that carpet makes her house feel warm and cosy, plus she likes to walk around her home barefoot. Her passage is painted in two different colours, terracotta at the bottom and cream at the top. The carpet is a shade of chocolate, going all the way to the top of the house. She has a large picture on her passage wall of herself and her children. Along the stairway walls are wooden carvings of different animals. Her kitchen, office, and lounge are all on the ground floor. Sandy works from home a lot, which she prefers. Her kitchen is spacious with large grey tiles on her kitchen floor. Her larder fridge, freezer, and cooker are all silver. Her worktops are grey marble to match, and a grey marble table set in the middle of her kitchen floor with eight white leather chairs. The walls are grey and white which descend to her patio doors that lead to a large and well-kept garden. As Sandy was cooking, her son Samuel came home from work. 'Hi mum,' said Samuel.

'Hi honey, how was work?'

'Yeah, it was okay, the same as usual. Dinner smells good! What are you cooking?'

'Lamb and rice' replied Sandy.

'Nice, how long will it be? I'm hungry.'

'About ten minutes.'

'Is Scott home yet?'

'Yes, he's in his bedroom playing Xbox as usual.'

Samuel is 25, and 6ft tall, with short wavy hair; he loves to push weights, giving him a lean build. He has his own IT telecommunications company and is very good at fixing computers and devices. Sandy saw Samuel's potential and helped him to set up his own business, its been running for two years now.

Sandy looked at the time and realised that it was 6.30 already; she had a shower and got ready for her date with Teddy. She decided to wear a nice black, tight-fitting jumper dress, which was just above her knees, with black sheer tights and black wedge knee-high boots. She then wore a purple fur waistcoat to finish off her look. She thought that tights were appropriate for the time of year. It was May, and there was still an evening chill in the air.

'You look nice, mum, where are you going looking so hot?' Cammy asked. Cammy aka Camilla was one of the twins; she has long curly brown hair, bright eyes, and straight features; she looks a lot like Sandy. Camilla has a very bubbly, feisty personality and loves to dance; she works for Selfridges as a make-up artist.

'I'm going on a date,' replied Sandy with a big smile. 'Where's Cass?'

'She's in her bedroom studying,' Cammy replied.

'Have you both eaten your dinner?'

'Yes, mum! We're not babies you know; we eat when we're hungry. So, who are you going on your date with?'

'My friend, Teddy.'

'Who's Teddy?'

'Remember that guy you saw me talking to when we went shopping last week?'

'That one who kept saying how much Cass and I look like you?'

'Yes, that one,' replied Sandy. 'What do you think of him?' she asked with a curious look, seeking her daughter's approval.

'Um, well I don't know him, but he dresses well for an old man.'

'He's not old,' laughed Sandy.

'Compared to you, mum, he's old,' replied Cammy with a smile.

'What time are you meeting him, mum?'

'Eight.' Sandy looked at her clock and realised that it was 8 p.m. Sandy quickly kissed Cammy on her cheek. 'Love you, babes, bye,' she called, as she rushed down the stairs and out the front door.

Chapter 2

Sandy's phone started to ring as she sat in her car; luckily, she had Bluetooth and her phone connected to it straight away. 'Hi, Teddy.'

'I'm here waiting, where are you?' asked Teddy, sounding quite agitated.

'I'm on my way, be there in two minutes!' replied Sandy, then she quickly hung up.

'He's lucky I'm picking him up,' Sandy thought to herself. Then she laughed and thought that it's a woman's prerogative to be late, so he'd just have to wait. Sandy pulled up outside the pub; Teddy walked up to the car and Sandy smiled as she thought he looked swag. He wore navy blue jeans and a white polo shirt, with a navy-blue matching leather jacket. A white Kangal flat cap and navy blue and white Adidas high top trainers completed his outfit. Teddy's eyes lit up when he sat in the car and looked at Sandy.

'Hi, beautiful,' he said.

'Hi, babes,' replied Sandy, still smiling.

'Look at those pretty white teeth, you're so pretty, you're pretty, pretty, pretty like wow,' said Teddy, smiling.

Sandy laughed. She liked Teddy's character, she found him amusing and intriguing.

'Thank you, and you look very dapper yourself. So, where are we off to this evening?' asked Sandy.

'Babes, anywhere you want to go, I'm all yours this evening,' replied Teddy, gazing at Sandy with an intense stare.

Sandy felt a sensation run through her body and smiled. Sandy had already decided earlier where she wanted them to go. It was a nice wine bar in Clapham called Cococabana. It was very cosy and had a look of the Caribbean. She had been there before with Caroline and Joan on one of their ladies' nights out, checking out the different cocktail bars and comparing them, as they do from time to time. Sandy felt that it would be a nice place for a date because it had little intimate areas which she felt was quite romantic. Sandy also liked the fact that they had a nice food menu.

'There's a nice cocktail bar in Clapham we can check out.'

'Cocktail bar, cocktail bar! I only do straight drinks like rum or brandy babes, I don't do this mixing and blending of drinks. What about a pub?'

Sandy laughed. 'I love cocktails, but you can drink rum or brandy if that's your desire. You do not have to drink cocktails just because it's a cocktail bar.'

Sandy found a parking space across the road from the Cococabana. Teddy got out and opened Sandy's car door for her. Sandy was very surprised; he had exceeded her expectations. She liked it very much and thought, 'What a gentleman'.

'Thank you,' said Sandy as she stepped out of the car.

'You're welcome, babes,' smiled Teddy.

Teddy looked at Sandy up and down.

'Wow, you look good, pretty lady.'

He took her hand and escorted her inside. Cococabana was dimly lit with candles on each table. They found a nice corner table and sat down. Both looked at their menu for drinks they fancied. Sandy ordered a Sugarcane Delight cocktail. Teddy however did not like anything on the menu.

'Do you sell straight rum?' he asked the waitress.

'Yes,' she replied.

'Well, can I have that with a bit of coke?'

'Would you like anything to eat?' asked the waitress.

'No, we're good for now,' answered Sandy.

'This is a nice place, babe, very posh, yes very posh! I've never been to a posh place like this before!' exclaimed Teddy.

Sandy thought it strange that Teddy felt that the wine bar was posh. It was nice but not posh.

'It's okay,' responded Sandy.

'Babes, I only go to pubs.'

'Pubs!' she exclaimed.

Sandy detests pubs. She thought that they were old and boring and for people with no class.

'Where do you take women on dates?' Sandy continued.

'Date, date, I don't do dates!' he replied, screwing up his face like the word date was taboo. Sandy looked at him, her jaw dropped, and her eyes opened wide; she said nothing.

'Babes, this is the first time I'm doing this kind of thing.'

'Okay,' said Sandy, still lost for words.

'So, now we're here face to face, this is time for straight talk, straight talk because I really like you, really like you, so, what is it you want from a relationship pretty lady?' asked Teddy.

Sandy raised her eyebrows; she was surprised that Teddy had posed such a question. She felt that women were more eager to know where they stood; this was a first for her.

'Well, umm, a man to be a man; a man who holds his own and is not dependent on a woman. Someone that my children can respect and turn to for advice; a man that I can enjoy and do things with.'

'Things like what, babes?'

'Like going out for a meal, or to the movies, or going away for the weekend. I would like to ring my man and he answers his phone or at least rings back at some point of the day.'

Sandy thought better than to mention marriage at this point.

'Well, babes,' responded Teddy, 'it's like this, I don't depend on anyone. I don't ask anyone for nothing. I have two brothers and two sisters, and I don't ask them for anything. I'm not going to lie to you, I've just got my place which I'm sorting out. I also have my children that I have to take care of, and I want to buy a car. Once I'm settled and sorted out my place, then I can be the man that I am. I don't let my woman spend her money; I like to look after my woman. I have two phones, babe, there's one and there's the other one.'

Teddy laid both phones on the table. 'If you ring one phone and you don't get me, then you ring the other. I must hear one of the phones and if not, an hour will not pass before I ring you back.'

Sandy liked what she heard; although she was puzzled as to why he would have two phones.

She felt it best not to ask. They both sipped their drinks.

'So how many children do you have?' she asked.

'I have seven children and five baby mothers.'

Sandy's eyes opened wide. She continued to sip on her drink, hoping not to show any form of expression.

'The third baby mother and the last one each has two children for me. I am close to all my children, anything they want, I get it for them.'

'Okay,' she replied, quite stunned. 'So, any twins involved?'

'No, no twins, no twins!'

'What are their ages?' 'The first is a boy is 32, then a daughter who is 25, and then a son and a daughter, one is 20 and the other is 18. Then another daughter who's 13. The last ones are two girls, one eight and the other one is six.'

'Okay,' Sandy replied still feeling quite stunned and speechless.

'Do you want another drink?' he asked.

'Oh, yes, thanks, the same thing please.'

Teddy ordered two more drinks, then looked at Sandy with a deep penetrating stare. Sandy disliked when men stared at her so intensely, she felt that they could read her thoughts which she did not want to share.

'You've gone quiet, babes, what's wrong, too many children?'

'No, it's not that. I mean, I've got five, so you only have two more than me. But no, I'm just surprised, that's all.'

'What are you surprised about?'

Sandy stared at her drink, then took a sip, Teddy stared at Sandy, waiting for an answer. Sandy felt his stare, she knew he wanted an answer, but she did not know what to say. To break the silence, she asked, 'So, what do you think of this place, do you like it?'

'Sandy, let me tell you something about me. I don't like anyone to take me for a fool or play games with me! I am a straight-speaking person so if you have something to say, just say it, don't beat around the bush!'

Sandy took another sip of her drink and looked up at Teddy; she disliked his continuous stare; he made her nervous.

'The truth is Teddy; I don't know what I'm surprised about. It's just that you have a lot going on.'

'What do you mean, a lot going on?'

'Well, it sounds like you're a terrific dad which I think is great, but you have a lot of things to sort out for yourself and I wonder where do I fit in? I mean, it does not seem like you have the time for a relationship.'

'Ha-ha!' laughed Teddy, 'Is that what you're worried about babes? Look at me.'

Teddy placed his hand on Sandy's chin and turned her face towards him.

'Babes, I love my children, they will always be a part of my life, but I need someone for myself. I will always find time for you, always babes, always.'

He then leaned forward and kissed Sandy on the lips. Sandy felt weak, a tingle shot through her body straight to her vagina. She loved it when a man took control, it left her feeling tingly and nervous all at the same time. She smiled and thought it best to take control of her emotions. She held her glass, tapping its side with her fingernails as she looked at Teddy.

'What else do you want to know, Sandy?'

'No, no, nothing but I was just thinking.'

'Babes ask me whatever you want. I've laid my cards on the table and I have nothing to hide.'

'Well, you say that you're fixing up your place, which would indicate that you recently moved in.'

'Yes, true, true,' replied Teddy, nodding his head.

'So, I am wondering if it's because you've recently broken up with your children's mother?'

'No, no, babes, none of that, none of that. It's because I've not too long come out of prison.'

'Prison?' she choked as she took a sip of her cocktail.

'You alright, babes?' he asked, as he patted her back.

'Um, yes, yes I'm fine thanks,' Sandy responded as she composed herself. 'So, how long were you in for?'

'Two years.'

'So, if you don't mind me asking?'

'Ask away babes, as I said I lay my cards on the table.'

'What did you go inside for?'

Teddy looked at Sandy, he rested his elbows on his knees and clutched his hands.

'It was a running's that went wrong, babes. I was trying to make some extra money for my family, but my friend and I got caught.'

Teddy shook his head and looked down. Sandy could tell that this was a touchy subject for him. She could see the pain in his eyes and decided to leave it well alone. There was a long silence; because of Sandy's profession, she knew that silence could be reflective and good for the thought process. It also gave her time to think about if she wanted to move forward with this relationship.

'She left me after I was sentenced. I'm not angry, I had a lot of time to reflect, and I suppose we weren't really getting on before I went inside. Still, I thought that she would be there for me.

'That's life though, babes, you can't trust people. Maybe it's because she's young, that's why I don't want to deal with no young gal again.'

'How young is she?'

'She is in her thirties. It's just one of those things though, babes. They say that age does not matter but maybe it does sometimes.' Sandy felt Teddy's sadness and knew that his memory of this situation caused him a lot of pain. She reached over and touched his hands; he looked up at her and held her hand.

'Sandy, I really check for you, I've liked you for years. I can see everything you're feeling in your eyes, babes.'

Sandy looked down; she knew that she was an open book and she found it hard to hide her emotions.

'Just give me a chance; you're the first woman I've spoken to properly since I've been out.'

'How long have you been out for?'

'Five months, babes, I haven't even had sex for over two years.'

'You haven't had sex since you've been out?'

'No babes.' Sandy raised her eyebrows, and a smirk came across her face which she could not hide. Sandy knew that her love of sex was her biggest downfall, yet she could not help it. A sharp sensation hit her vagina and she became instantly wet. She knew that sex was a must, even if she did not have the relationship. She decided to play it cool, but Teddy had already read it all over her face and he began to smile. Teddy sat upright and looked at Sandy.

'Babes I've been straight with you, straight, I've told you everything, babes, everything. So, it is up to you now to be straight with me. Do we go forward from here or what?'

Sandy looked intently at Teddy and observed every feature of his face. She loved the shape and fullness of his lips. She liked how his eyes squinted when he smiled. She also liked the thickness and the natural shape of his eyebrows. The strain of life showed on his face and the sadness in his eyes. Sandy thought about how to play this. She did not want to be the rescuing mother, which was often her mistake in relationships. Caroline's words resonated in her head about her choices of men. Sandy did not want to offend Teddy, yet she liked the boldness of his character. She decided to choose her words very carefully.

'Well, Teddy this is our first date and although we have known each other for a long time, we are now starting to know each other differently. I respect how open and honest you have been with me. The trust that you place in me to relay such personal information.'

'Look, Sandy,' interrupted Teddy, changing the tone of his voice and looking at Sandy intensely.

'I've been straight with you, straight! So now I need you to be straight with me. Don't talk to me like I'm one of your clients, because I don't like that, don't like that, babe. None of this bull-shit respect and honesty crap, just straight talk. Do we go forward from here or not?'

Sandy lowered her eyes. She felt a burning sensation in her cheeks. Teddy took hold of Sandy's hand and stroked it with his thumb. Sandy looked at Teddy and smiled; she felt nervous, but she liked how forthright he was. She felt that if he put all that passion into sex, it would be explosive and passionate all in one. Sandy sat up straight and looked at Teddy, asserting control over herself and her emotions.

'Okay, babes, I hear you. I do like you, and I would like us to take our time and get to know each other some more. It sounds like you have a lot to sort out in the short time that you have been out of prison. So, let's continue to date and get to know each other and we can take it from there.'

'Okay, pretty lady!' responded Teddy with a smile, nodding his head. 'Sounds good, sounds good, yes, I do have a lot to sort out, but I will still find time for you. Plus, you're introducing me to these posh places that I like. So, anything you say babes, anything you say.'

Teddy and Sandy finished their drinks, he paid the waitress and they left.

'What you are doing for the weekend?' he asked, whilst Sandy was driving.

'Um, I'm going to this club over north, babes.'

'What kind of club?'

'Big people tings, different sounds or DJs from back in the day alternate every week. I do like my bashment but occasionally I like to do old skool.'

'So, what day are you going up there?'

'Friday,' replied Sandy.

'So, who are you going with?'

'Most probably my daughters, Cammy and Sophie.'

'Are they the twins I saw you with the other day?'

'No, I'm going with one of the twins and my eldest.'

'So how old are they?'

'The twins are 21, my eldest is 28.'

'I like that babes, I like that, too much of the friend ting ain't good. I like how you enjoy yourself with your daughters. I might come with you, something different; you don't mind do you, babes? If you do, just say because I don't want to impose myself on you and your daughters.'

Sandy laughed. 'No, it's cool, babes, I don't mind at all.'

Sandy pulled up on Prentis Street to drop Teddy off.

'I really enjoyed this evening, babe, call me when you get in. I want to know that you reach home safe.'

Teddy leaned over and kissed Sandy. He softly sucked her tongue and her bottom lip. Sandy relaxed her mouth, leaving his mouth and tongue to take control. He then looked at Sandy with a stare of lust and passion.

'I wish I could come home with you, babes; I love these juicy lips.' Teddy then held Sandy's neck and stroked it with his thumb and kissed her more intensely. Sandy leaned back and let out a deep groan. She felt weak, her vagina was throbbing.

'I want to make love to you,' he whispered in her ear.

Sandy felt breathless and started to breathe heavily. She put her hand on the back of Teddy's head and kissed him back passionately. Then she slowed down the kissing and pulled back.

'Okay, babes, okay, babes, maybe we should stop now.'

'Stop, babes! I have not had sex for over two years, I want to fuck you right now, feel it babes, feel it, feel how hard it is.'

Sandy put her hand on his groin and felt how big and hard he was.

'You feel how hard it is, babes, you feel it?'

'Yes, I feel it, babes, I feel it, but not tonight,' said Sandy in a gentle tone. 'I have to get up early, I will see you Friday.'

Teddy held Sandy's face and stared into her eyes then he kissed her softly on her lips.

'Okay, whenever you're ready. Call me when you reach home.'

'Yes babes, I will,' replied Sandy.

Sandy could see Teddy watching her as she drove off. 'I could have fucked him right there,' she thought, 'but it's too early, it won't look good, I have to give it some time. They say a month for people in their forties, but I've known him for a long time so maybe I don't have to wait that long.' Sandy's thoughts were interrupted by her phone ringing, it was connected to her car phone.

'Hi, Ras,' she said.

'I've been ringing your phone all evening, what the fuck is wrong with you, Sandy, have you not seen my missed calls?'

Sandy wanted to laugh; she forgot that she had put her phone on silent.

'Sorry, babes, I was with Caroline, I forgot that I had my phone on silent, you okay, babes?'

Ras kissed his teeth.

'Where are you now?'

'I'm in Streatham, on my way home, babes.'

'Well swing by and pick me up, I'm at the studio,'

'I have to be up really early,' she responded.

'So, do I, babes, just come for me. I miss you.'

'Okay, I'll be there in ten minutes, make sure you're ready, cause I'm not going to sit and wait for you.'

'Oh, stop your noise and just come, you're so miserable, man, I'll be ready.'

Sandy looked at her car clock and saw that it was 11 p.m. 'I'm hardly going to get any sleep, but I'm horny as hell,' she thought to herself.

Ras was waiting outside the studio when Sandy arrived. He got into the car and looked at her.

'Why do you give so much trouble? You see you never had to wait for me?'

'Yes, this time! You're on time for once, so what, you want a trophy?'

'You're so cheeky and miserable,' responded Ras. 'It's because I haven't given you a good fuck in a long time.'

'Whatever. What are you doing in the studio?'

'I'm just laying down a few tracks with my friend. I was ringing you for about an hour straight, why you never answer your phone?'

'I told you, I was with Caroline, and I forgot that my phone was on silent.'

'So why was your phone still on silent when you finished work earlier?'

'How do you know what time I finish work?' replied Sandy with a raised voice. 'Furthermore, you know that I work from home. So as long as all my children are home, I don't need to watch my phone.'

'So, what you are doing in these ends when you live in Purley? Where you coming from?'

'Why all the questions?' responded Sandy.

Ras knew that Sandy had to pass her house to drop Caroline home, she was glad that she was driving so that she did not have to look at him. She hated lying and she knew that if he looked into her eyes, he would see that she was lying.

'Look, I've had to deal with something with Caroline and I'm not going to chat her business to you.'

'So, where is Caroline?' asked Ras, looking seriously at Sandy.

'I dropped her off at her man's house, he will drop her home.'

Sandy felt hot and uneasy, she was happy when she pulled up in her driveway. She did not like being questioned. She remembered that she had to ring Teddy.

'Go on up to the bedroom, babes, do you want a drink?'

'Yes, give me a glass of that fruit punch you make with some ice.'

'Okay,' Sandy replied.

Sandy watched Ras climb the stairs then she went into the kitchen and quietly closed the door behind her.

'Hi babes, I've just reached home, have you reached home yet?'

'Yes, pretty lady, I've just reached home, I can't stop thinking of you, you're constantly on my mind, I need you in my life, babes, in my life.' Sandy smiled.

'I've been thinking of you too, babes, it was a lovely evening, but I'm really tired,' Sandy yawned, 'I have to be up really early'.

'Okay, babes, okay, get some rest, I'll speak to you in the morning.'

Sandy liked Teddy and she knew that she had to end the relationship with Ras at some point, but she did not know when.

'Here's your drink, babes, get off my bed with your outdoor clothes! You know that you should take off your trousers before you sit on my bed.'

'Sorry, sorry, I forgot, my clothes are clean anyway, I freshened up before I left the house,' replied Ras in an apologetic tone.

'Yes, then you've been sitting in the studio. I don't want no bugs biting me in my bed whilst I sleep!'

Ras rolled his eyes but said nothing and started to undress.

Sandy went to the bathroom and freshened up before getting into bed. Sandy relished that she had an en-suite bathroom. She could lock her bedroom door and relax in her own little kingdom, without her children being in her business. Ras was already in bed when Sandy entered the bedroom. She smiled and curled up in bed next to him. He held her in his arms and began to kiss her passionately. Sandy knew that she had missed him. She loved his strong arms and firm chest; he turned her on as soon as he touched her.

'You missed me, babes?' he whispered, as he started to kiss her neck, then breasts, going straight to Sandy's nipples.

He held her breast with one hand and sucked and nibbled on her nipple. Sandy let out a groan and opened her legs further as an acknowledgment of his question. Sandy lifted his face and started to kiss him passionately. She licked and sucked on his ear lobe. Ras stroked her vagina.

'You've shaved, I like that.'

He gently stroked her vagina then pushed his finger into her.

'You're so wet, you're dripping.'

'That what happens when you leave me without sex for so long,' she responded.

Ras parted her legs even further to penetrate her.

'Take your time with pushing it in, I don't want to tear.'

'You're so wet, you won't tear.'

'You're too big, babes; I always tear when we don't have regular sex. You have the condom babes?'

'Let me just wet my tings in your pussy juice first.' He then pushed his penis inside her vagina.

'Mmm,' responded Sandy. 'put the condom on.'

Ras pulled out and reached for the condom. He felt good inside her, but Sandy knew better than to sleep with him without a condom. Sandy knew that although Ras slept with other women, he was very responsible. It had taken him a whole year before he attempted to have sex without a condom with her. Nevertheless, Sandy was not going to take any chances with him. He puts it on.

'Turn round, babes,' Ras urged.

She crawled to the end of the bed and bent over. His favourite position. Ras loved doggy style; he placed the pillow under Sandy's chest and positioned her with her head on the mattress and her arse up in the air. He rubbed some of the lubrication jelly into her vagina before penetrating her. Ras pushed his penis deep inside her, stroking her vagina back and forth with his penis. Sandy started to pulsate, she grabbed a pillow and placed her face in it to muffle her screams, she did not want her adults to hear her. She orgasmed one after the other.

'You're so fucking wet, girl, talk to me, babes.'

'Fuck this pussy hard, honey, fuck me hard, you're making my pussy so wet. You're making my pussy vibrate for you.'

Sandy did not like talking dirty, she liked to remain quiet with her thoughts. All kinds of thoughts and fantasises ran through her head during sex, but she knew that for Ras to come he liked her to talk dirty. Ras would only come when he knew that Sandy had reached multiple orgasms, Sandy liked this. She knew that he wanted to please her, and he was not a selfish lover. Letting out a groan, she felt the vibration of his penis as he was coming. They both smiled at this result. Sandy curl up in his arms and they both fell asleep.

Chapter 3

Sandy awoke and looked at her clock, it was 8.30 a.m. and her first client was at 10 a.m. She went to the bathroom and stepped into the shower. As the water touched her vagina, she felt a sharp sting. 'Oh fuck, I've torn!' she exclaimed to herself. Ras was awake when Sandy came out of the shower with her blue towel wrapped around her. He looked at her and smiled.

'Ready for round two?' he asked.

'You think I've got nothing to do but to fuck all day? I thought that you had to get up early and go to work.'

'Yes, but I'm waiting for a phone call. I'm hungry. Make me a coffee and an egg sandwich, please.'

'You fuck me the fuck off, honestly!' exclaimed Sandy.

'What's your problem?' retorted Ras.

'I told you that I had to be up early.'

'So, your client is coming to your house, it's not as if you have to go on the road.'

'That's not the point, I like to feel relaxed before I see anyone. I don't like to feel rushed and bothered!' snapped Sandy.

'I've noticed from the other day, you've been acting funny, I'm not stupid, you know Sandy, you women think that because you have your fancy education that you can tek man for fool, but I'm no fool, Sandy!'

Ras was interrupted by the vibrating of Sandy's phone. She picked it up and saw that Teddy was ringing her. She did not answer it, the phone stopped then started to vibrate again. Ras looked at Sandy; she could see the lines forming on his forehead.

'Who is it? Why don't you answer your phone?'

'It's an unknown number, I'm not answering no unknown number. So what time are you leaving?'

'I'm leaving in a bit, babes, can you please make me a cup of coffee, I'm hungry, I gave you some good sex last night, so you need to feed me,' he said, smiling and rubbing his stomach.

Sandy said nothing, she was annoyed and frustrated, she wanted Ras to leave but she was trying her best not to offend him; she got dressed. She wore a purple fitted v neck dress which was just below her knees. The sleeves were three-quarter length, with a silver chain and matching earrings. She did her make-up and hair. Sandy loved that her hair was short, it was a lot easier to manage.

Sandy went to the kitchen to make breakfast. Cammy was sitting at the table in her nightwear.

'Morning, honey, no work today?' asked Sandy.

'No, mum, you forgot it's my day off; so how was your date?' asked Cammy with a big smile.

'Um, it was good, he seems okay.'

'You don't sound too excited.'

'Well, man is man, who knows, things always seem good in the beginning, so I'll see.'

'Okay, well I'm going back to bed and get out of your way before your client comes.'

Sandy had thought that all the adults would be out of the house; she did not want any of them to see Ras. She knew that none of them liked him, they had made it clear on many occasions. Especially Cammy who continuously verbalised her dislike of him. Sandy knew that they were right with their assumptions of him. They felt that he was a liar, a cheat and was no good for her. Sandy wanted Ras to leave early so that none of the household would see him. She wanted to keep her business to herself. Sandy hoped that she could get him out of the house before Cammy saw him. She made Ras his coffee and egg sandwich and brought it to him.

'Look, babes, my client is coming in a bit. I'm going to prepare for her, so now just relax until I've finished then you can leave.' She turned around and rolled her eyes that she was compromising with him again.

This was a repeated scenario with Ras. Sandy was fed up with Ras saying that he would leave early, then making excuses. She would not have mind if Cammy were not home. She was frustrated that Ras had put her in the predicament again of one of her adults seeing him.

'So, how long will you be?'

'It's just a 50-minute session; my next client is at 12. I will drop you up the road when I'm finished.'

'Cool, I'm just gonna relax and watch some news.'

'Do you want anything else from the kitchen?'

'No, maybe we can have round two when you come back up.'

'You're so fucking annoying! For one, I tore, two, I'm busy working; which you should be doing as well.'

'How you tear? You were really wet plus I used the lubricating jelly.'

'You know this is what happens when we don't have sex for a while, it's not as if you're small.' Ras smiled at this remark.

'I'll take my time and push it in.'

He then grabbed Sandy and pulled her onto the bed.

'Let me go!' protested Sandy.

Ras climbed on top of her and pinned Sandy's arms above her head. Sandy fought back in vain.

'Look Michael, you're pissing me off! My client will be here in 10 minutes, I have no time for your foolishness.'

'Just two minutes, that's all, I won't even come I just want to feel your wet pussy.'

Ras stared deep into Sandy's eyes, then, whilst holding her hands with one hand, he pushed the other hand between her legs. He pulled her knickers to one side and pushed his finger into her vagina.

'Your pussy is so wet!'

He then stroked his finger back and forth. Sandy relaxed. He kissed her deeply, sucking her tongue whilst fingering her. Sandy opened her legs further allowing him to take control. Sandy kissed him back passionately. He then relaxed and let go of her hands. Sandy held his face and looked at him.

'Babes, you know you always turn me on, and I want to feel you inside me. As soon as I'm finished with this client, I'm all yours,' she said in a soft, warm voice.

'Okay, babes, hurry up and come back,' replied Ras, as he eased himself off her body.

Sandy got up, straightened her clothes, and checked herself in the mirror. Ras stood next to her and rubbed her arse.

'You look good, babes; I could stay in bed and fuck you all day.' Sandy looked at Ras and smiled.

'Of course, you could, babes, of course of you could,' she replied as she walked out the door and went downstairs.

Sandy knew that it was pointless fighting with Ras. She had to start work. Sex was the last thing on her mind, she needed to get Ras out of her house before Cammy saw him.

Sandy finished with her client. She went into the kitchen to make herself a drink; Cammy was sitting at the table eating a salmon bagel.

'Mum why is he here, I thought that you weren't going to see him anymore?' Sandy felt Cammy's annoyance in her voice.

'I know, I know, I hoped that he would be gone,' replied Sandy, feeling like a child being scolded by her mother.

'Look, mum, your private thing is your private thing, I understand, but I walked in here and there he was in the kitchen making himself a drink! I was so shaken, why was he in here?'

'He was making himself a drink?' asked Sandy.

'Yeh, why does he always like to act as if he's man a yard, as if he pays rent or something? I thought you went on a date last night mum. You're not gonna meet anyone good if you keep that loser around!'

'Okay, Cammy, I hear you.' Sandy walked out, annoyed and went upstairs to the bedroom.

Ras was sitting on the bed watching TV; he turned and looked at Sandy as she entered the room.

'You finish now?' he asked.

'Yes, for now,' replied Sandy, 'Why did you go down to the kitchen?' She questioned as she sat down on the chair opposite her bed.

'What's wrong? I went to get a drink. Then Cammy walked in, the look she gave me was not good. What, she said something?' he asked, looking concerned.

'Michael, I live with my children, and not all the time I want them in my business. I only agreed to you coming last night because you said that you had to be up early.'

'Yeh, but I did not receive a phone call saying that I had to come in today!'

'I asked you what you wanted before I saw my client so that you would not have to go to the kitchen.'

'So, what you saying, I can't go to the kitchen for a drink if I'm thirsty?' replied Ras, raising his voice.

'I'm saying that I don't want my children in my business. I would have preferred Cammy not to have seen you.'

Ras stood up and started to get dressed.

'You're letting your children rule you. Furthermore, they're not children, they're adults. You need to take charge in your house!'

'That's not the point. They know that you don't treat me right. They know that whenever I ask you to help me with something, you disappear. They just want the best for me.'

Ras kissed his teeth.

'Just drop me up the road let me go about my business. I have no time for this crap! I went to get a drink; I don't see what the problem is.'

Sandy wanted to ask him if he provided drink money, but she thought better of it. She grabbed her car keys and pulled on her black suede boots and her black leather jacket. Ras followed her out to the car, they both walked in silence.

On the way back from dropping off Ras, Sandy remembered Teddy. She had received 10 missed calls. She knew that he was going to question her about not answering her phone. Sandy decided to speak to him after she saw her next client. She arrived home and went to her office to await her client. Her office was cosy with cream walls and beige deep-pile carpet on the floor. Her desk was placed in front of her window which faced the garden. There were two black chairs in the middle of the room. She had a picture of sunflowers on one wall. She kept the room simple so that the client could focus more on the session instead of the room. She sat in her black leather chair and reflected on the situation with Ras. She understood Cammy's feelings concerning Ras although at the same time she could relate to what Ras had said regarding her children ruling her. She felt that her children were now adults and what she did was her business. Sleeping with Ras was not affecting them. Yet, at the same time, she knew that her children loved her and wanted to see her happy. Sandy knew that they knew that he did not make her happy. She thought about what she would say to a client in her situation. She would help the client to gain an understanding as to why they continued to prolong such an unhealthy relationship. If it were her friend, she would want to be the rescuing mother by telling her friend to stay away from him because he's undeserving of her. 'Why am I, therefore, continuing this relationship?' she asked herself. Her thought pattern was distracted by the doorbell, her client had arrived.

Chapter 4

Looking forward to tonight, mum?' asked Sophia, standing by her kitchen sink washing up.

Sophia is Sandy's eldest daughter; she has a brown complexion and she's petite with long locks flowing down her back. She loves to wrap her locks in different styles. Sophia has two girls, Diamond age 6, and Candy aged 4. Sophia is a teacher, but she gave up work about two years ago to home school her daughters, whilst her partner Danny works as a builder.

'Yes, I suppose; my friend Teddy is coming with us if you don't mind?'

'Whose Teddy?' responded Sophia, turning from the sink to look at Sandy.

'It's this guy whom I have known for a few years. He claims that he has liked me for a long time. We went on a date a few days ago.'

'So how was the date?' Sophia asked.

'Um, it was alright I suppose. I mean a date is just a date, I don't get excited over these things anymore, it is what it is,'

Sophia dried her hands and sat down at the kitchen table with Sandy.

'You don't sound that excited, mum, talk the tings!' said Sophia in jest whilst smiling. 'There's something you're not telling me; I can see it in your eyes.'

'No, it's nothing much,' responded Sandy with a grim look.

'Mum, just say what it is.'

'It's just that he seems to have a lot going on. He has seven children, which is okay, only that the last two are around the same age as Diamond and Candy whilst his eldest is older than you,' sighed Sandy.

'I know you always say that you don't want a man who has children under the age of ten.'

'That's the thing, Sophia, what I find is that no matter if the man is in his forties or fifties, he has young children plus grandchildren. I just don't understand these men.'

'Yeh, I get what you're saying, mum,' replied Sophia, nodding her head in agreement.

'I mean,' continued Sandy, 'I would like a guy that I can do things with, like going away for weekends or on holiday. These guys still have to do school runs.'

'Plus, too much baby mama drama!' laughed Sophia.

'Exactly!' exclaimed Sandy. 'Total foolishness. It's as if these men don't want to grow up. Plus, he's been inside and has only been out a few months.' Sandy turned away from Sophia, feeling a sense of embarrassment.

'Okay, well what did he do?' asked Sophia.

'I don't know, he said a running's that went wrong,' replied Sandy.

'How long was he inside for?'

'Not that long, a couple of years, I think.'

'Well, as long as he did not kill anyone or beat no woman, I suppose.'

'No, nothing like that,' responded Sandy.

'Do you want a drink, mum? I have some rosé,' smiled Sophia.

'Yes please, I need one,' responded Sandy, smiling back.

Sandy found it easy to speak to Sophia; she was not judgemental; she would just listen. Sophia also wanted the best for her mother, like the other siblings. Sandy knew that her daughter trusted her to make the right choice in the end. Sandy felt that maybe because she had left home and had her own family, she saw things from such a different perspective.

Sophia picked up two glasses and poured some wine then went into her freezer for ice.

'So mum, what do you actually like about this Teddy?'

Sandy's eyes lit up and she smiled.

'He makes me laugh. When he speaks, he has to say everything twice; I find him amusing. Plus, he's good looking and a snazzy dresser. He's always complimenting me which is nice.'

'Oh mum, please, you're always getting compliments!'.

'Yes, but it's nice when it comes from someone that you like.'

'So, does this mean no more Ras?' asked Sophia.

'Ras is Ras, here today, gone tomorrow. He was around the other day; Cammy did a flip mode'.

'Yeh, she told me,' laughed Sophia.

'The whole thing annoyed me. I mean, Cammy is old enough to know the score and Ras should have kept his arse in the bedroom. Before I picked him up, I told him that I was busy and had to be up early and he said that he also had to be up early. I thought the fool would leave before anyone saw him,' said Sandy shaking her head.

'But mum, he always does this; it's as if he does not want to leave once, he comes to spend the night.'

'Yes, true, you're right but I made him breakfast and asked him if he needed anything else, he said no; so, I don't know why he had to get up and go to the kitchen, he's just too much.'

'He gets too comfortable, that's why. Plus, you know what Cammy's like,' responded Sophia.

'Yeh, you're right on both counts. Anyway, I have to love you and leave you. I need to get my nails done before the shop gets packed, you know what Fridays are like.'

Sandy finished her wine.

'Yep, true, you better hurry. What time are we leaving, and who's driving?'

'I thought 10.30 is good, it takes about an hour to get there. I'll drive if you want, just come by mine and jump in my car; where are the girls?'

'They're upstairs, I gave them some colouring to do; Diamond, Candy, your nan is leaving!' shouted Sophia.

Diamond and Candy rushed down the stairs 'Nana, Nana, where you going, can we come with you?' asked both girls in sync. Sandy hugged the girls and laughed.

'No, not today, your nana's very busy but I will take you out soon. I left some sweets on the kitchen table for you.'

'Yay!' exclaimed the girls and rushed into the kitchen. Sandy kissed Sophia on the cheek.

'Thanks for the wine, honey. I needed that.'

'It's Friday and I don't have to cook,' thought Sandy, smiling to herself as she stepped through her front door. Sandy did not mind cooking; she felt it was important for her children to have a home-cooked meal. But now that they were adults, Sandy was tired of cooking every day.

'Hi, mum, what's for dinner?' asked Scott whilst walking down the stairs. Sandy rolled her eyes.

'Leave me, Scott, it's Friday, you know I don't cook on Fridays.'

'I knew you were going to say that I just knew,' laughed Scott.

Scott is 6 ft 5 inches tall; he has long cornrows down his back. He loves pushing weights. He and Samuel try to out-do each other. Scott is very jovial and loves to joke around. He is in his final year at college, studying games design. Sandy feels that gaming is his best route because he's always playing Xbox and he wins a lot of tournaments.

'So mum, are we having Chinese today?'

'Yes, we can, I just need to see what everybody else wants,' replied Sandy.

'Well, I'll have my usual, King Prawn Chow Mein,' said Scott.

'How was college today?' asked Sandy.

'It was okay, same as usual, they just keep talking to us about university because it's our final year. I'm not interested in university; I'd rather find a job or an apprenticeship after college.'

'I don't know why they keep pushing this university thing down students' throats. Unless you're going to study a profession, it's best to try and find a job and get some work experience in the area of your choice first. Then you can go to university at a later date if you still want to,' responded Sandy.

'I know, that's how I feel. University is not for everyone and it's not for me right now!' replied Scott.

'Cass is at university because she's studying law, which is a profession. Just focus on passing the course and look at your options.'

'Evening, mum,' said Cassandra, interrupting the conversation.

'Hi honey, nice to actually see you,' replied Sandy.

'What do you mean, mum, I'm here every day,' responded Cassandra.

'Yes, you are, Cass, but you're always locked up in your bedroom.'

'It's true, sometimes I forget what the rest of this house looks like,' laughed Cass.

Cassandra is 21 and is identical to Cammy; her hair is shoulder length with curls and dyed copper red as a way of owning her own identity. Cassandra is a no-nonsense, straight-talking person; she believes in equality and justice and constantly defends her beliefs. Which is why Sandy agreed that law was her best option. Cammy is a lot feistier than Cassandra; she is direct and not afraid to speak her mind. They are both very protective of Sandy.

'Cass, can you please tell mum what you're having for Chinese? I'm hungry, and mum won't order until she knows what everyone wants,' said Scott hastily.

'Mum I don't know why you do this every week; you know what everyone likes, just order the same things,' retorted Cass.

'Well, I know that Cammy wants the same as me. Singapore noodles and Sweet and Sour King

Prawns but Samuel may want something different.' Sandy paused to think.

'Mum just order the same as mine, he will be happy to have food,' Scott sighed.

Sandy realised that Scott was getting agitated, she knew he was hungry.

'Okay, okay, I'll order now,' responded Sandy.

Later, Sandy stood at her wardrobe looking at her clothes, wondering what to wear. She was fortunate to have a walk-in wardrobe, every item was neatly in place. The trousers and tops were on one side and dresses, skirts, and blouses on the other side. In the centre were her shoes and jewellery. Above her clothes, she placed her handbags, scarves, and hats on the shelves on either side. She decided to wear her white slim-fit jeans and a red sleeveless v- neck fitted top. Tonight, was casual smart so she thought it best to wear her red diamante sandals. She then looked at her jewellery and decided to wear her silver choker, with matching earrings and bracelet. Sandy laid the items on her bed and went to shower. She then did make-up, got dressed and sprayed her perfume for the finishing touches. Sophia walked into her bedroom.

'Wow, mum, yes I like!' exclaimed Sophia.

'Thanks, babes.'

Sandy turned and looked at Sophia, she was wearing a white cold shoulder summer dress which was just above her knees. Sandy smiled and looked Sophia up and down.

'You look really nice; I love the dress. You just need a lovely chain to bring off the dress.' Sandy walked into her wardrobe and looked at her chains.

'Well, mum, that's why I came to your room first. I knew that you would have a chain that I could borrow.'

'You girls think that I'm a shop. I keep saying that when you're buying clothes think of matching jewellery - that's how you build your collection.'

Sandy then picked a three-tiered pearl and gold choker. 'This will suit what you're wearing. Turn around let me put it around your neck.'

Sophia turned, she looked in the mirror.

'I like it, mum, very nice,' said Sophia, smiling as she looked at herself in the mirror.

The ringing of Sandy's phone startled her.

'What's the time, Sophia?'

'It's 10.40.'

'See what Cammy's up to please. I told Teddy that I would pick him up at 11.00, we need to be leaving now.'

'Hi Teddy, you, okay?' asked Sandy as she answered the phone.

'Yeh, I'm good babes, good. Just checking that you're okay and you're still picking me up for 11.00.'

Sandy chuckled to herself; she knew that she was not going to be on time.

'See you in a bit, babes,' she responded and then hung up.

'Cammy are you ready, I'm leaving now!' shouted Sandy.

Cammy came downstairs wearing an all-in-one short-sleeved multi-coloured bodysuit. Sandy admired her daughter's shape; she was curvy with a small waist.

'You look nice and firm, honey. You're young so you carry it off well, I like it,' said Sandy, admiring her daughter.

'Plus, mum, her make-up matches the blue, yellow and red patterns, um, I'm impressed,' said Sophia, looking at Cammy and smiling.

'I am a make-up artist, guys, remember, but what I do not have is a chain to match,' said Cammy looking at her mum and smiling.

'Go choose one and let's go,' said Sandy, grabbing her clutch bag and shawl.

'Okay mum, I'm coming!' Cammy cried out.

'Don't forget to turn off my bedroom light and close the door!' Sandy shouted whilst she walked down the stairs.

'So where are we meeting this, Teddy?' asked Sophia, getting into the car.

'What, what, did you say Teddy?' interrupted Cammy.

'Yes, mum's friend Teddy is coming with us, she's picking him up,' responded Sophia.

'Wow, hold up, mum, you never told me that Teddy was coming!'

'Yes, sorry I forgot to tell you,' replied Sandy.

'So, does this mean that I can't sit in the front of the car?' responded Cammy.

'Oh, stop your noise Cammy and sit in the back next to me. So, mum where are you picking him up?' asked Sophia.

'In Norwood,' replied Sandy.

'That girl gets on my nerves sometimes,' Sandy thought to herself whilst driving. Sandy loved all her children very much, but she found Cammy exhausting at times. She wished that Cammy would be more relaxed and mind her own business, but she always felt the need to control situations. This annoyed Sandy sometimes. Sandy knew that it was because she had a close relationship with her children, and she did a lot of socialising with them. This was the reason why they felt that they had some form of authority in her private life. It was difficult because she liked to party, and Caroline did not party because of her faith. Joan only liked old skool raves, which Sandy found boring at times. It's not that Sandy did not have friends, she had Monica and Lorraine too. But she found that once her friends had met their partners and married, they pulled away and their friends became other couples. Sandy was left with her daughters to party with, which she enjoyed, but had to therefore contend with the intrusiveness, especially from Cammy.

Sandy knew that she was also to blame because she spoke to her daughters about situations, she was experiencing which made them feel protective of her and they therefore reacted at times. She felt that their reaction was unnecessary because she was able to handle her own business. Sometimes, their actions made her feel as if she were the child and they were the parent. There were times when she felt that she had to fight for her position as a mother and take back control.

'Mum, I'm connecting my phone to your car, I've got some nice Alkaline tunes for you to hear,' said Cammy.

'Alkaline, yes I love his music, I love his voice and his style!' exclaimed Sophia.

'I hope Teddy likes this music and if he does not, too bad. I hope you don't start turning down the music when he gets into the car, mum!' said Cammy, whilst rocking to the music.

'Shut up and play the music Cammy. Teddy loves bashment!'

Sandy pulled up across the road from the Kentucky, she was 10 minutes late. Teddy was standing on the other side of the road. He stared at the car then took his time to cross the road. Cammy sucked her teeth.

'What's his problem? He's lucky that you're even picking him up. Mum, you should just drive off and leave him there!' exclaimed Cammy.

'Just cool, Cammy, and don't say anything when he gets into the car,' responded Sandy.

Cammy said nothing, she just kept the music volume high. Teddy got into the car and looked at Sandy. Sandy turned down the music.

'Sophia, Cammy, this is Teddy.'

Teddy turned around and looked at the girls.

'Hi princesses, nice to meet you'.

'Hi,' replied Sophia.

Cammy was messing with her phone, but she looked up and said a quick 'hi' then continued messing with her phone.

'Sorry, I'm a bit late babe, traffic,' said Sandy apologetically.

'It's okay, you're here now,' responded Teddy.

Sandy turned up the music volume to settle Cammy but made sure that the volume was at a level so she could converse with Teddy.

'So how are you, babes? I've missed you, been thinking of you all week,' said Teddy whilst staring at Sandy.

From her peripheral vision, Sandy could see Teddy staring at her which made her blush.

'Been good, just busy working but I've been looking forward to seeing you also.'

'You did not have to wait for tonight to see me, babes, you could have seen me anytime, babes, anytime. Just call me and I drop everything for you, everything, it's because you just don't know how much I check for you,' said Teddy with a big grin.

Sandy laughed, she liked Teddy and hoped that the girls would like him too. She thought that once they all got into the club and had a drink and started dancing, they would like his character and hopefully, they would all have a good time.

'We're finally here!' said Sandy as she parked her car.

Teddy held her hand as they walked to the Culture Club, Sophia and Cammy looked at each other and said nothing. Sandy liked what Teddy was wearing; he wore black Versace trousers, with black Versace sneakers, a white Ralph Lauren polo shirt, and a black Givenchy bomber jacket. Sandy smiled; she loved his style although she thought that he had really expensive taste.

'You look really good,' said Sandy, looking Teddy up and down.

'Not as good as you, but we look good together,' replied Teddy.

Sandy smiled.

'How much for the four of us?' Teddy asked the cashier.

'£20,' she replied.

'Are you sure? We can pay for ourselves,' said Sandy.

'It's cool, babes, relax, I've got this,' replied
Teddy as he paid the cashier.

'Not everyone is as broke as Ras,' whispered
Cammy to Sophia and Sandy whilst Teddy was
paying.

'True. Get used to it, mum.' Sophia voiced.

The club was very spacious, the bar was
located at the side of the wall near the entrance,
the DJs were on the other side of the wall
opposite the bar. The speaker boxes were huge
and were placed by the adjacent wall near the
entrance door.

'What you all drinking?' asked Teddy.

'We will all have a Magnum, please!' Sandy
replied.

Sandy knew the girls would want a Magnum;
they always ordered the same drink whenever
they went to the Culture Club. Teddy brought
Sandy and her daughters a Magnum each and
handed it to them.

'Thank you, and nice to meet you,' said Sophia
with a smile.

'That's cool, I have big children like you two. I
feel as if I'm out with my own daughters, so don't

worry, I'm here to look after you all!' Shouted Teddy over the music. Sophia nodded and smiled.

'Thank you!' shouted Cammy whilst holding up the drink and nodding her head. Teddy nodded back.

'Thanks, babes,' said Sandy close to Teddy's ear so she did not have to shout. Teddy smiled and gave her a quick peck on the lips.

They found a nice spot adjacent to the DJ stand and began to rock to the music. The DJ played 'No Man Is an Island' by Dennis Brown.

'Oh, I love this song!' exclaimed Sandy.

Sandy put one of her hands up in the air and began singing to the song.

Teddy looked at Sandy and smiled, putting one arm around her waist and the other arm around her shoulder, then he placed his forehead on hers. He moved slowly one step at a time whilst moving his pelvis against Sandy's pelvis. Sandy placed her arms around his waist and followed his movements. Sandy could feel Teddy's penis starting to swell. If this had happened with a man that Sandy did not know, she would have stopped dancing and walked away; but it was

Teddy, and she liked the fact that she gave him an erection. Sandy continued to brace against Teddy and whine. When the song finished, Teddy looked at Sandy and smiled.

'You're a bad girl,' he whispered in her ear. Sandy laughed.

The DJ then played 'Sitting in The Park' by Cassandra. Sandy held on to Teddy and continued to whine, her pelvis against his. Teddy held on to Sandy, and they both whined in sync together.

'You're a good dancer,' Sandy said to Teddy.

Teddy looked at Sandy and smiled.

'So are you, babes, so are you, you can whine. I like that, I like that, but right now babes, I'm hot.'

Teddy stopped dancing, took out his rag from his back pocket and wiped his forehead.

'Don't they play any upbeat music, babes?'

'Yes, they do,' laughed Sandy, 'Why, don't you like these types of music?'

'They're okay, long time music, don't they play any bashment? I prefer bashment, babes. '

'I told you what type of music they play. They do play some bashment, but this is more of a culture night, big people, tings.'

Teddy gave a grim look and continued wiping his forehead.

'Do you want a next drink?' Teddy asked Sandy.

'No, I'm good, thanks.'

'I'm going outside to smoke, be back in a bit.'

Teddy held Sandy's hand and gave it a little tender squeeze then went outside to smoke. Sophia and Cammy moved closer to Sandy.

'Where has he gone, mum?' asked Sophia.

'Outside to smoke. He does not like the music, he prefers bashment.'

'I know how he feels. I have to have a drink to contend with some of the music which is so old,' said Cammy whilst finishing her drink.

'Yeh, but you're young, Cammy, he needs to flipping grow up. He must think that he's a teenager or something,' said Sandy, looking unimpressed.

'Leave the man alone mum, he likes what he likes!' interrupted Sophia.

'Um, I suppose. Do you two want a next drink?' asked Sandy.

'Yes, please, I'll have a Magnum again,' replied Cammy.

'So, will I,' said Sophia.

'You two better mind; you know that Magnum is a creeper.'

Sandy went to the bar and brought Sophia and Cammy a Magnum each, and a bottle of water for herself.

The DJ changed the genre to reggae, playing 'King of The Dancehall' by Beenie Man. Teddy walked towards Sandy and began dancing in front of her. Sandy smiled; she liked the way he moved. The DJ continued with this genre of music. Sophia and Cammy began to whine and bend over to the tunes especially when the DJ played 'My Dream' by Nesbeth. The crowd cheered so much he had to restart the song about four times. Sandy laughed when she saw Sophia whining. Whining is more Cammy and Sandy's style; Sophia is a lot more conservative when dancing. 'Yes, Sophia, do your thing!' shouted Sandy still laughing, Sophia laughed and continued to dance.

'You know she's gone, mum,' laughed Cammy.

'I know, good for her, she needs to free up and have fun,' replied Sandy, smiling at her girls. 'Teddy loves dancing!' shouted Sandy to Cammy and Sophia. Cammy laughed.

'Yes, he does, I see him about the place doing his gully creep,' laughed Cammy.

Sandy laughed; she knew that Teddy loved to dance.

Sandy thought about Ras. She had been to the Culture Club with him a couple of times; she loved that Ras enjoyed any type of music. She remembered when she first met him at Silvarna night club where she went with Joan and Sophia. Ras was standing near the bar; he could not keep his eyes off her as she stepped through the door. Sandy saw him but ignored his stares. She did not find him attractive and did not want to encourage him to approach her.

A tall, slim, brown-complexioned man had approached Sandy and asked her for a dance.

Sandy thought that he was attractive and danced with him. That was the first and last dance Sandy had had with him. She did not like the way he held her and squeezed his fingers in her back whilst pushing his pelvis against her. The DJ started to play 'Rare Groove'. Sandy smiled and danced. Ras approached her and held her hand gently and asked her for a dance. She danced with him because she liked his approach. He held her gently and she loved how he danced so smoothly. She continued to dance with him for the rest of the night.

'You look lost in thoughts, babes, what's on your mind?' asked Teddy as he placed his arm around her waist and began to dance. Sandy smiled.

'Oh, nothing, babes, you seem to be enjoying yourself. The music is to your taste now I presume?' replied Sandy. Teddy stared into Sandy's eyes.

'I'm good, babes, I'm good,' then he smiled and kissed her. 'I want to come home with you, I want to fuck you, then make love, then fuck you again, babes. You turn me on so much, so much. I feel like I could explode here right now, honestly, honestly.'

Sandy's vagina started to pulsate; she loved the power her sexual energy had over men. She wanted to fuck him so badly but one part of her wondered if it was too soon. The other part of her did not care, life is too short, just live. Sandy placed her arms around his neck and looked into his eyes, Teddy smiled. Her vagina felt so wet that fucking was not a choice, it was a necessity.

Sophia swayed from side to side whilst trying to walk straight. Sandy held onto her to stop her from falling as she walked Sophia to her front door.

'Mum, mum can I tell you something?' whispered Sophia to Sandy whilst trying to walk straight.

'Yes, Sophia, you can tell me anything,' replied Sandy.

'Well mum I, I, I just need to tell you that I love you very, very much.'

'Yes, I love you too, Sophia.'

Mum, I also have to tell you!' Sophia began to laugh hysterically.

'Shush, Sophia, you're going to wake up the street.'

'Shush,' replied Sophia, putting her index finger on her lips, 'Mum I have to tell you something.'

'Yes, Sophia what is it?' replied Sandy in a weary voice.

'When I get inside mum, when I get inside, I'm going to fuck Danny, mum, do you want to know why mum, do you want to know why?'

Sandy chuckled; she knew that Sophia would be so embarrassed in the morning.

'Why, Sophia?' replied Sandy.

'Because I am so horny, mum, so, so horny!' Sandy was just about to place the key in the lock when Danny opened the door.

'Magnum?' asked Danny.

'That's the one,' replied Sandy, smiling.

'Danny, Danny do you know what I want to do to you?'

'Yes, I do, and so does the whole street. Goodnight, mum, by the time she hits the bed she'll be out cold.'

'She's not usually like this at all,' explained Sandy to Teddy as she got back into the car, feeling quite embarrassed. She hoped that Teddy had not heard what Sophia had said.

'It's cool, babes, it's cool,' replied Teddy.

Sandy did not know what to make of his statement as he showed no expression.

'You okay, Cammy?'

There was no response. Sandy looked behind her, Cammy had fallen asleep.

'She drop asleep long-time babes, long time from you step out the car with your daughter.'

'Well one down, just one to go,' said Sandy.

'Yes, then I can have you all to myself, babes.'

Sandy smiled; she still did not know if it was a good idea to let Teddy come home with her. It was okay when she was feeling horny but now that her libido had calmed down, she was not too sure.

'So, what are you up to tomorrow?' asked Sandy.

'I'm quite busy tomorrow, babes, I'll be gone from early. I have a few tings to sort out, is that cool with you?'

Sandy was happy with his response; she did not want her adults to see him before being properly introduced.

'Yes, that's okay, so how did you like the Culture Club?'

'It's okay, not bad, not bad, at least they changed the music to a more upbeat selection. Even your daughters were bored at first, I could see it in their faces,' replied Teddy.

'Um, I suppose, I mean they know how the music is. It starts with some revival then it changes to a more upbeat style. It also depends on the DJs on rotation, different DJs have their own style. I enjoyed myself, it's good to be versatile.'

'Babes, I know all dem music from long time I used to move with King Tubby's and Frontline sound years ago. When I go out, I like to dance. I'm not into that rub up, rub up ting that you like. I like to free up myself and dance. I'm not saying that I don't like dancing with you, don't get me wrong, babes, but I prefer to do my own thing.'

Sandy was not impressed; 'That's why I always go back to Ras,' she thought to herself, 'he's versatile and fun.'

'You've gone quiet, you don't like what I said?' asked Teddy.

'It's okay, babes, you are your own person, and you have the right to like what you like. Now I know that you prefer to dance on your own, and that you're not into revival music, I now know how to flex with you.'

'So, what do you mean by that?' asked Teddy.

Sandy could sense Teddy staring at her, she sensed he was becoming agitated by the change of tone in his voice. She felt frustrated with him but thought it best to change the mood of the conversation.

'I mean that I know that you prefer bashment. I could see that you love dancing. You're a very good dancer, by the way. I would rather go to dances with you which I also enjoy, so we can enjoy them together'.

Teddy's expression changed and he began to smile.

'Yeh, that will be good, we can definitely, definitely go to a dance together then you will see me in action! I did enjoy dancing with you though, babes. A man would be insane, insane, did you hear me? I said insane, babes, if he did not like dancing with you. It's just that you love the whining ting, you whine to everything babes. At least with me, you will stop whining so much.'

Sandy smiled and said nothing. She realised that he did not like her whining because it took the attention away from him. Sandy knew that the problem lay with Teddy and his insecurities, and she was not going to take them on; she would continue to dance how she wanted whether he liked it or not.

'I've never met a man who had a problem with the way I dance. Men always compliment me.'

'That's because when they watch you whine; they're only interested in one thing. I know what I'm talking about, babes. I'm a man and I know the way men think.'

Sandy thought better than to entertain Teddy any further, he had jealousy and control issues and she knew she would have to tread carefully.

'Cammy, Cammy, wake up, we're home now, babes!' Cammy staggered out of the car and Sandy held on to her.

'I'm okay, mum, I'm okay! I can walk, just open the front door, mum.' Cammy staggered up the stairs.

'Goodnight mum, love you.'

'Love you too, Cammy, goodnight.'

Teddy followed Sandy into the house. 'Would you like a drink?' asked Sandy as she walked into the kitchen and turned on the light.

'Why, what do you have?'

'You can have a hot drink or some juice, whichever you prefer.'

'Don't you have anything stronger?' replied Teddy as he sat down at the kitchen table.

'Um, I have white rum or brandy.'

'Yeh the white rum, babes, the white rum, what juice do you have to chase it with?'

'I have orange or blackcurrant juice.'

'I'll have the blackcurrant juice.'

'Would you like ice?'

'No! No ice babes, no ice. You have a nice house though, it's big and spacious,' said Teddy, observing the kitchen.

'Thank you,' replied Sandy whilst getting herself a glass of water.

'You're not drinking anything stronger?' asked Teddy whilst sipping his drink.

'No. I only drink water when I'm going to bed. Are you ready to go upstairs? You can bring your drink.'

'Am I ready, am I ready, me ready long-time babes!' replied Teddy with a big smile and giggle whilst he followed Sandy upstairs and into her bedroom.

'Just one thing, babes, I don't allow anyone to sit on my bed when coming from outside.'

'Babes, I don't sit on beds, I don't sit on beds. When you get to know me better you will see that I am a very funny person, very funny. Certain tings I don't like babes, I don't like. I am a very clean and tidy person, very clean and tidy.'

Teddy sat on the chair near the window and placed his drink on the small mahogany side table. Sandy went into the bathroom to freshen up and change her clothes. She brushed her teeth and removed her make-up. 'What am I doing?' Sandy thought to herself. 'I'm not sure that I want to sleep with him let yet alone have a relationship with him.' She took a deep breath and sighed. 'Oh, well, it is what it is. Life is short, let me see where this takes me,' she said to herself. She changed into her red spaghetti strap vest top with matching red shorts.

'Hi, sexy lady,' said Teddy smiling as Sandy walked out of the bathroom.

He walked up to her and pulled her by the waist close to him. He kissed her and sucked on her bottom lip. He played with her lips with the tip of his tongue.

'I want you, babes. I'm just going to use your bathroom, warm the bed for me.'

Sandy smiled and pulled down her bedsheets, she dimmed the lights with the remote control by her bed. Sandy had a king- size bed with a chocolate brown padded Camargue headboard.

Her bedsheets and pillowcases were Egyptian lilac cotton which matched her purple duvet.

Sandy felt both excited and nervous. She was attracted to Teddy, and he sexually turned her on. She smiled when she saw the bathroom handle go down and Teddy walk out. He had on a white vest and white Calvin Klein boxer shorts. Sandy admired his body, she loved how his legs looked strong and firm like a footballer. His shoulders and arms were a lot more defined than she would have anticipated for a man in his fifties. He got into the bed and took off his vest and placed it on the chair beside the bed. Teddy took Sandy into his arms then held her face and sucked on her lips.

'Stick out your tongue!' demanded Teddy.

Sandy stuck her tongue out, Teddy sucked on her tongue. He began to breathe heavily; he kissed her face and neck.

'Take these things off,' ordered Teddy as he tugged at her top.

Sandy sat up and pulled off her top. Teddy took it from her and dropped it on the floor beside the bed. He then pulled at her shorts.

Sandy lay down and lifted her bum and pulled down her shorts as his actions suggested. Teddy pulled them from her legs and dropped them on the floor. He pulled off his boxer shorts. Sandy opened her legs. Teddy sat on his heels between her legs and looked at her.

'I love your breasts, babes,' said Teddy as he played with her nipples and felt the fullness of her breasts.

He rubbed his hands up and down her body until he reached her vagina, he looked into her eyes. Sandy closed her eyes.

'Open your eyes, babes. I want to look into your eyes whilst I'm touching you.'

Sandy opened her eyes and looked at him. His finger rubbed up and down Sandy's clitoris. Sandy bit onto her bottom lip. She saw Teddy's penis rising stiff, the veins on his penis looked as if they were about to explode.

His penis was thick and big, ready, and waiting. He slowly pushed his finger into Sandy's vagina and stared at her. Sandy let out a deep moan and arched her back, easing her vagina up towards his finger. Teddy looked at Sandy and smiled and stroked his finger back and forth into her vagina.

'Umm! Fuck, this feels so good,' Sandy said as she began to suck on her finger and look into his eyes.

'Your pussy is so fucking wet, if I don't fuck you now, I'm going to explode.'

Sandy picked up a condom from her bedside table.

'Babes put the condom on,' said Sandy, handing the condom to Teddy.

'I don't need any condom. I had all the checks in prison, every check you can think of. I have not slept with anyone since I've been out, you're the first to get all this, babes,' replied Teddy as he held his penis. 'I need to feel the inside of your pussy. I have not been inside a pussy for a long time. Are you okay?'

'Yes, I'm okay', replied Sandy, breathing heavily.

'Well, say no more, babes, said Teddy as he took the condom from Sandy and threw it on the floor.

Sandy squealed as he pushed his penis into her. He held up both her legs with his arms and opened her legs even further. He rode in and out of her like power punches. Sandy grabbed a pillow from beside her and placed it over her face to muffle her screams. She felt his penis vibrating, he arched his back as he released.

'Thank you, Lord, thank you,' cried Teddy. 'Your pussy is amazing, fucking amazing.' He flopped onto the bed beside Sandy. He turned her face towards his and kissed her.

'You are good, babes?' asked Teddy.

'Yes, I'm good,' replied Sandy.

Chapter 5

Sandy was woken by muffled sounds. 'I was trying not to wake you, babes.' Teddy had finished dressing and was getting ready to leave. 'I have a lot to do today, plus I have to visit my son and daughter, I will ring you later.'

Sandy got out of the bed and wrapped her towel around her body.

'Yes, okay babes, I'll just follow you to the door,' replied Sandy, yawning.

'Go back to bed, you're tired. I know where the front door is.'

'I know, I'm just going to make myself a hot drink then I will go back to bed,' replied Sandy.

Sandy walked wearily down the stairs behind Teddy, holding on to the banister with each step. Teddy kissed Sandy on the cheek.

'I'll call you later, go back to bed,' whispered Teddy.

Sandy smiled and locked the door behind him and went back to bed.

Sandy is very protective of her home and children; she would not be able to go back to sleep until she had seen Teddy leave and made sure that her front door was secure. She knew that Teddy would have been offended if she had been honest with him. She did not know him well enough to trust him; plus, she was not sure about him altogether.

The sun shone brightly through the curtains of the bay window. Sandy stirred then opened her eyes. 'I need to remember to buy black-out curtains,' she thought. 'Oh shit, it's noon already!' she exclaimed as she looked at her bedside clock. Sandy did not like to stay in bed past 10 o'clock unless she was on holiday. She has her Saturday routine. Put clothes in to wash, then clean her meat or fish for Saturday and Sunday dinner, then start cooking. Every Saturday she spent at least three hours in the kitchen which she hated but continued to do.

Sandy went into her bathroom and stepped into the shower. She let the warm water flow over her body. 'This feels so good,' thought Sandy. She took the hose and opened her legs and washed her vagina. 'No stinging, no tear,'

Sandy smiled to herself. Whilst getting dressed Sandy could hear her phone ringing; it was still in her handbag.

'Hi, Teddy.'

'I've been ringing you straight for the last ten minutes, have you not seen the missed calls?'.

'I was in the shower and the phone was in my handbag.'

'Just now you waking up?'

'Yes, it is Saturday, and I was tired!' replied Sandy feeling quite agitated.

'Okay. Cool, cool, I was just checking on you. I had a nice night, babe. I want to see you again. Last night was just a quick ting. I don't want you to feel that I'm a man who comes quick, plus I was drinking. I want to make love to you properly. What you up to later?'

'I don't even know, Teddy. I've not too long woken up; I will call you back later.'

'Okay, you do that. I have a dance that I might go to later. So, if anything, I will check you in the early hours, call me later.'

'I will,' Sandy replied.

'This man seems too possessive; I don't like it. He must think that my phone is stuck to me. I don't know why he thinks that I'm even interested in sleeping with him again,' she said to herself.

Cassandra was already in the kitchen cooking herself some lunch.

'What are you making? I'm hungry,' said Sandy.

'Oh, hi mum, I'm just frying dumplings and plantain and warming up some baked beans, want some?'

'Yes, thanks.'

Sandy looked at the kitchen counter and drawers.

'Cass, why do you have to make so much mess when you cook? There's flour everywhere.'

Sandy took the kitchen cloth and began cleaning up the mess.

'Mum it's not that messy and you know that I will clean up. You've got OCD, that's your problem.'

'I have not got OCD. I just don't like mess, especially unnecessary mess. All you have to do is take the flour and put it in the bowl, it's a very simple task!'

Cassandra ignored Sandy and dished out some food for her. She knew better than to argue with her mum about cleaning up the mess. Sandy made herself lemon and hot water to drink and sat at the table and ate.

'So how was last night?' Cass asked Sandy, changing the subject.

'It was okay. Teddy is a strange character,' Sandy replied, staring at the wall with a blank expression.

'What do you mean strange?' asked Cass as she joined her mother at the table.

'He has a subtle controlling nature, which I'm observing.'

'I don't understand, elaborate mum.'

'Well, he continuously rings my phone until he gets me. Then when he does, he questions me on why I have not answered his calls.'

'That's a bit full on so early, mum. How long have you been seeing him?' Cass asked Sandy, with a curious look on her face.

'Not long at all, only a couple of weeks if that,' Sandy continued 'Then he has a way of questioning my character, in a way that makes me doubt my actions.'

'Mum, you're the therapist, sometimes I wonder where you meet these men. Just think about what you would say to a client in this situation. What do you like about him?'

'I'm beginning to ask myself that same question,' replied Sandy.

'So did Sophia and Cammy enjoy themselves?'

Sandy began to laugh.

'Sophia was buzzed. You know how Sophia does her little elegant dance until she gets drunk?'

'Why, what was she drinking?' interrupted Cass.

'Magnum,' replied Sandy, smiling.

'Well, that's it then mum, how much did she drink?'

'Around two or three.'

Cass started to laugh 'Okay mum, give me the joke, what happened?'

'You should have seen her in the club backing it up.'

Cass laughed.

'She was totally gone by the time I reached her house; she was making so much noise on the road. Letting the neighbours know how much she wants to fuck Danny.'

'No way,' laughed Cass, looking quite shocked.

'Danny opened the front door. She woke him up,' said Sandy, still laughing.

'Oh shit,' laughed Cass, 'she's going to feel so ashamed when she wakes up. I have to call her. So, what did Teddy say?'

'He did not say anything. I just hope that he did not hear what she was saying but I'm sure he did.'

'So, how was Cammy?'

'Cammy's Cammy, always dancing and loud but by the time I got back to the car after taking Sophia to her front door, Cammy was out cold.'

'She still is, I have not heard a peep out of her all morning,' Cass responded.

'I like the fact that he's not mean, he paid for all of us to get in and brought us drinks, which was nice,' said Sandy.

'That's the norm, mum, it's just that Ras is such a broke arse.'

'I know, that's what you all keep telling me.'

'That's because it's true, mum. When is the last time he took you out?' asked Cass.

Sandy went silent. Cass stared at her, waiting for an answer. Sandy shrugged her shoulders, got up from the kitchen table and started to wash up. She knew that Cass was right. The truth is Sandy had only been on an actual date with Ras twice, and that was when they had just met, and he had been trying to impress her.

'I need to tidy this kitchen so that I can start preparing dinner and seasoning this chicken for tomorrow.'

'That's why we call him a broke arse, mum' said Cass, placing her plate in the sink.

'So, what are your plans for today?' Sandy asked Cass, changing the subject.

'I'm going to do a bit of studying, and then Kevin is taking me out on the town later,' replied Cass with a big smile on her face.

Kevin is Cassandra's boyfriend; she has been seeing him for about a year. They met at university where he also studies law. Sandy likes him because he treats Cassandra well and is always spoiling her with gifts. She can see that her daughter is smitten with him. Sandy knows that she needs to settle with a man that her children can respect. She taught her children principles and values. Which is why she could never settle down with Ras.

Sandy stood at the kitchen sink and cleaned her fish; she decided to cook steamed fish with okra, green banana, yam, and dumplings. She steamed some rice because Samuel and Cammy did not like yam or green banana. She would have preferred everyone to like the same thing instead of having to cook different dishes. Sandy wished that she had not spoilt them from they were young and demanded that they ate what they were given otherwise stay hungry. She then smiled and said to herself that you can't force people to eat what they don't like. She thought about what Cass had said about Ras which echoed what Sophia and Cammy had also said last night. I have to end this with him once and for all,' thought Sandy. 'I cannot tell them one thing and do another.' Sandy seasoned the fish and started to clean the chicken.

'Afternoon, mum,' said Samuel as he walked into the kitchen.

'Afternoon, honey, you hungry?'

'No, I'm good, I had something whilst I was out. I had to go into work to check on some new equipment.'

'So how are things going?' asked Sandy.

'It's going okay, I got a new contract with a school which is good.'

'That's good,' smiled Sandy.

'So, what's for dinner?' asked Samuel.

'Steamed fish with….'

'Steamed fish,' interrupted Samuel, 'are there bones in it?'

'It's just one bone in the middle, Samuel, you need to stop acting like a baby. Just take your time and eat it, you can't have meat all the time.'

'Okay, so when are you cooking the chicken?'

'Tomorrow, Samuel.'

'Is there not enough chicken for me to have some today and tomorrow?'

Sandy rolled her eyes.

'I'm not paying you any mind, Samuel. Leave me alone, let me finish doing what I'm doing and don't bother me.'

'You're tired?' asked Samuel.

'Yes, Samuel, I'm tired. I need to make you all take turns to cook on a Saturday. You're all old enough now.'

'Mum, if you need some help just ask.'

'I should not need to ask; you all should just offer to help.'

'What would you like me to do?'

Sandy turned and looked at Samuel, 'Well. thanks for offering, you can cut up the onions, peppers, and tomatoes for me, please.'

Sandy felt exhausted after cooking and decided to go to her bedroom and lie down. She had dozed off when her phone rang and woke her. Sandy saw that it was Ras. She decided to let it ring out. One minute later, the phone rang again, and it was Teddy. Sandy wanted to ignore the call, but she knew that Teddy would continue to ring her until she answered.

'Hi, Teddy.'

'What you doing, babes, sleeping?'

'I dozed off, what's up?'

'I'm good, just want to hear your voice. What have you been doing all day that makes you so tired?'

'I was cooking, plus I'm still a bit tired from last night.'

'Was thinking of checking you later, around 4 a.m. on my way back from a party.'

'I don't think that that's a good idea', Sandy replied.

'Why, are you going out?'

'No, I will be asleep and I'm not going to wake out of my sleep to answer the door! Plus, my children do not know you and they will all be home. I cannot let them see a man that they do not know in my bed.'

'Your children are not babies, just let them know who I am!'

'So, who are you, Teddy?' responded Sandy, slightly raising her voice.

Sandy waited for a reply, she heard nothing; she knew that Teddy had not hung up the phone because his name still appeared on the screen. Sandy knew that Teddy was temperamental and that raising her voice may have not been the best way to express her feelings. She was tired and felt annoyed at his persistence, she was also uncertain if she wanted to start a relationship with him. Sandy waited for him to respond, she heard the traffic in the background, yet still no reply.

'I'm going back to sleep so I will speak to you later.' There was still no answer, Sandy hung up the phone.

Chapter 6

'HI Peter.'

'Good morning Sandy, you look bright and chirpy this Thursday morning.'

'Thank you, Peter,' replied Sandy, smiling.

Peter is Sandy's supervisor, and she sees him once a month for supervision. He has a small office which Sandy feels is warm and cosy. His desk is situated near the far wall in front of the bay window, which has a white floral pattern net curtain and cotton blue lined curtains that match the blue carpet. The walls are pale blue. The leather chairs are placed diagonally across from each other so that the sun cannot shine on either of their faces during the session. Sandy likes Peter, he's tall with a dark complexion and bald head. He always wears a suit, which Sandy admires. Sandy feels that his suit makes him looked distinguished. She loves his wide smile which shows his white teeth.

'So, how have things been since I last saw you?' asked Peter, looking at Sandy whilst adjusting his glasses.

'It's going good with my clients; my personal life is another thing. I notice that I continuously keep getting clients who are in a similar situation as myself or who have been through things which I have experienced.'

'Is there any particular client that you would like to discuss with me today?' Peter sat cross-legged with his writing pad on his lap and pen in hand.

Sandy admired his shoes, black leather laced Samuel Windsor with tan leather sole. She loved shoes and she knew quality when she saw it. Sandy opened her writing pad.

'Client A is a 45-year-old black woman, she has two children a boy aged 13 and a girl aged 16. Her partner is 10 years younger than her she has been with him for about a year. He sleeps out sometimes and does not contribute to the household consistently. Although she is not happy, she does not want to leave him because she does not want to be on her own.' Sandy looked up at Peter and smiled. 'I want to tell her that she's already on her own and that he is full of shit, and she should kick him out.'

'I sense resentment and anger, Sandy; what feelings does this situation bring up for you?' asked Peter.

'I feel angry because at one time I was weak and accepted things that I should not have,' replied Sandy, lowering her eyes.

'So, you feel that because she is not addressing her situation the way you feel that she should then it's a sign of weakness?'

Sandy sighed, 'I suppose.'

'Well, there's a couple of things going on for you, Sandy. You felt hopeless in your situation but because you're stronger now, you have never forgiven yourself for allowing such a situation, which I'm sure was traumatic. The other thing is your need to be the rescuing mother. Your client is not your child, Sandy. She is your client, and she is going through her own processes just like you had to go through yours.'

Sandy looked at Peter and nodded.

'Yes, you are right. I try my best to suppress my feeling when counselling her, being aware of transference.'

'That's very important, Sandy. We will always meet clients whose issues will resonate with some of our issues but it's important to recognise them during the sessions. Always remember that it's about the client, not you.'

Sandy nodded in agreement.

'What you need you to do, Sandy, is forgive yourself. It's not weakness, it's a next person abusing kindness.'

'You're right. I cannot continue with this emotion every time a client or situation makes me remember what I went through and how I felt.'

'Sandy, if you're used to handling pebbles, then one day you will come across a rock and you will find that it is too heavy for you to handle. In time you will get stronger and when you do, you will be able to move the rock. It's not weakness, Sandy, it's time.'

'You know, Peter, I never thought of it that way.'

'This woman has come to you to gain her strength which is buried within her for whatever reason. It's for you to help her find that reason. In time, she will gain her strength so that she will be able to handle the next rock if she ever bumps into one again.'

Sandy smiled. 'I like your analogy, Peter; I will use it with my clients if you don't mind.'

'It's okay, I'll let you have that one for free,' Peter chuckled.

'Now, what's going on with you?' asked Peter, uncrossing his legs.

Sandy liked talking to Peter about her problems, although he was not her therapist. She felt that he challenged her, which helped her to look at her situation with new eyes.

'In our last meeting, we spoke about the choices you make regarding relationships and ending with Ras. Have you ended the relationship with Ras?'

Sandy lowered her eyes and smiled. 'Well, yes and no.'

'Yes and no is not an answer, Sandy,' replied Peter looking at Sandy over the rim of his glasses.

'I have decided to walk away although I have not exactly told him straight out, plus I'm kind of seeing someone else who I'm not too sure about.'

'You have a lot going on here, so let's backtrack a little. You say that you have decided to walk away from Ras, but you have not told him? It sounds as if you're unsure whether to end the relationship with him or not. Tell me, how do you feel about Ras, Sandy? Before you answer, I want to hear about your feelings not what your children or what your friends think about him. I want to know your feelings.'

Sandy rested her head on the back of the chair. Peter looked at Sandy, waiting for an answer, his face expressionless. Sandy was usually very good at reading people, except for her supervisor. She found it difficult to read his thoughts. Sandy lifted her head and looked at Peter.

'I do care about him. I like his charisma; he is fun to be around. He makes me laugh, plus the sex is great.' Sandy smiled as she thought about the sex., 'I have not told him that I no longer want to see him because I feel that I will just be repeating myself. Plus, I never felt that we were exclusively in a relationship.'

'Sandy, you have expressed more than once what you would like from a relationship, yet you continue to date men who have not grown into men. You are a good therapist, Sandy, and the reason why you attract men who have not grown up is that you need to grow up within yourself.'

Sandy's eyes opened wide, she stared at Peter.

'I do not accept that, Peter. I am a grown woman. I just make silly choices because I try to see the good in the bad and try not to be judgemental.'

'Sorry if I offended you. I know that you're a woman who holds her own. What I'm trying to say is that as a woman, you know what to do. You are a responsible person. You raised your children on your own and they are doing very well. When I say grow up, I'm referring to the way you view men. Fun and great sex are wonderful in your twenties, but when you're in your forties or fifties, it's about being responsible.'

'I understand that' replied Sandy, 'which is why I no longer will continue a relationship with Ras.'

'Yes, Sandy, but you should have not started a relationship with him in the first place. A woman does not need to tell a man how to be a man, his actions will show you who he is.' Sandy listened and said nothing. 'You're a very beautiful woman inside and out. You're independent, have your own business, own your own house and car. It's not easy for some men to match up to you.'

'Which is why, Peter, I try not to be judgemental because I know that it is not easy for the black man in England.'

'Yes, Sandy,' replied Peter, nodding his head. 'but you are not their mother, you have your children to raise. A man does not have to be on the same level as you to be a man, his actions are what makes him a man. Our time is running short now, so just think about what you want and don't accept anything less.'

Sandy went to Café Nero, a short walk from Peter's office on the high street. This is her routine and every month after supervision, she goes for a cup of hot chocolate and a strawberry and white chocolate muffin. She likes to take time out away from home to think about her session. Sandy knew that her supervisor was right, she felt as if she had just been told off by her father. This was a strange thought because Sandy was estranged from her father and had not spoken to him in years.

Sandy's parents had separated when she was seven. She had a very close relationship with her father, so she was devastated. Her father had married the woman with whom he had cheated on her mother, and they had three children. Her stepmother had never accepted Sandy or her siblings. Her father was so besotted by his wife that he was blinded and never saw how she treated his children.

'It's not about liking the person, it's if that person is good for me. Both Ras and Teddy are not good for me,' Sandy said to herself. Sandy was so lost in deep thought that she did not see or hear the tall black man standing on the opposite side of her table.

'Seems like you're lost in deep thought,', chuckled the man, holding a cup of hot beverage and a panini. 'You don't mind if I sit here?'

'Oh no, sorry, I did not hear you, yes sit down,' replied Sandy whilst adjusting herself in her seat.

'I didn't mean to startle you,' said the man, placing his cup and plate on the table opposite her. 'It's just that there are no more seats, it gets quite full in here sometimes.'

Sandy noticed his deep dimples and bright, wide eyes. He wore a yellow florescent vest and looked a little dusty.

'I know I look a mess. I work on the building site across the road.' Sandy smiled. 'Sorry to intrude, you looked deep in thought,' the man continued. 'I'm Shaun, by the way.'

'I'm Sandy, you'd better sit down and eat your panini before it gets cold.'

Sandy was not in the mood for chit chat, she had a lot on her mind, although she thought that he was handsome. Sandy thought it best to finish her hot chocolate and took a sip, screwing up her face.

'Don't like your drink?' asked Shaun.

'It's okay,' replied Sandy, 'just a bit cold.'

'Would you like another one?' he asked.

'No, I'm fine, thanks for asking.'

'I've seen you in here before, a few weeks ago, it's nice to see you again,' said Shaun with a big grin. 'Not that I've been stalking you or anything but it's not difficult to notice a beautiful, elegant, black woman.'

Sandy smiled but felt awkward and surprised, as she has never seen him before.

'Yes, you're probably right, I come in here once a month,' she said.

'Well, I'm glad to have seen you again. So, is there any particular reason why you only come in here once a month?'

'I see my supervisor once a month, his office is nearby. I come here afterwards to reflect on the session and just to have some time out for myself.'

'I feel guilty now for disturbing you, no wonder you were so lost in thought,' said Shaun.

'How long before the new apartments are finished?' Sandy asked him.

'We still have about six months left, it may seem quite finished from the front, but we still have all the back to complete. So, Sandy, what do you do?' he asked, whilst taking a bite of his panini.

'I'm a therapist,' Sandy replied. Shaun nodded his head, finishing what was in his mouth before he spoke.

'Sounds very interesting. I did not realise that therapists have supervision, why is that?'

Sandy smiled. She liked his response; most other guys usually asked her to give them counselling.

'Supervision is mandatory whilst seeing clients. Plus, it helps me to know that I am on the right track with my clients, and I am working ethically. I also find it useful to do role play with my supervisor as this helps me to have a deeper insight into my clients' issues.'

Shaun stared at Sandy attentively, taking in every word.

'I'm sorry,' said Sandy, 'I can get quite carried away when speaking about counselling.'

'No, no, don't apologise,' replied Shaun, wiping his mouth with his napkin. 'I can tell that you love what you do, your face lights up whilst you're speaking. I've always been intrigued about counselling, and you explain things very well.'

Sandy blushed, and lowered her eyes. She liked his energy, it felt genuine.

'Thank you, Shaun, it was nice speaking with you, but I do have to go now.'

'It's been nice speaking with you too, Sandy. I don't want to sound pushy, but I would like to see again outside of this coffee shop, perhaps take you out for a meal. I find you interesting. Would it be okay to have your number?'

Sandy was speechless for a moment; she had enjoyed the conversation but was unsure if she should give him her number.

'I don't bite, just a meal or drink, your preference.'

Sandy smiled. 'I'll take yours.' She passed her phone to Shaun. Shaun took the phone and tapped in his phone number.

'Thank you,' said Shaun, returning her phone. 'I hope to hear from you soon.'

Sandy thought that he was a good-looking man and he seemed genuine and polite, but she was not sure that she wanted to meet anyone new.

She was fed up with both Ras and Teddy and felt that she needed some time to herself. Meeting someone new was far from her mind at this present time.

Sandy's phone rang just as she sat in her car. She looked at her phone and saw Teddy's name. She had not spoken to him since Saturday.

'Hi,' she said.

'Hi pretty lady, been thinking about you babes, thought that it would be nice to see you, want to link up later?' asked Teddy.

'I'm surprised to hear from you. I thought that you decided not to speak to me anymore.'

'No, no, no babes, nothing like that, nothing like that, me not talk to you babes. No way, why would you say a ting like that, babes?' replied Teddy.

Sandy smiled to herself and shook her head. 'Because the last time we spoke you were silent on the phone and did not respond to me.'

'That's not me, babes, I would never not respond to anything you ask me, anything. I remember I was going to check you but then my phone died. I did not hear what you said, and I was not able to ring you back. I was out and I did not have any way of charging my phone until I reached home,' responded Teddy. Sandy looked at the name on the phone and wondered if she was talking to Teddy or someone else.

'If that's the case, babes, then why did you not ring me back later that day or even yesterday? Plus, I thought that you had two phones.'

'Look, babes, why all these questions? I told you one ting, so what you trying to do babes, call me a liar? I don't like it, babes, don't like it. I told you my phone died and that's that. So, do you want to see me later? Because I want to see you.'

Sandy shook her head and laughed to herself; she knew that he was lying but she thought it best not to pursue this avenue of questioning.

'So, what would you like us to do later, Teddy?' asked Sandy, grinning.

'Anything, babes, anything you want to do, just name it.'

'Well, we can go to the movies or out to eat?'

'Money isn't running like that now. I thought that I could check you, it would be good to meet the rest of your kids.'

Sandy shook her head, unsure how to respond.

'I met your two daughters the other night, I thought that it would be good to meet the rest,' Teddy continued.

Sandy thought about her answer. 'So what time are you thinking of coming?'

'Well, I've got a few things to do, so is 7 okay?'

'Yes, 7 is okay.'

'Alright, babes, see you in a bit.'

'This man is strange; I know he heard every word I said which is why he wants to come to my house to meet them. I don't know how I get myself into these situations. Sex is my biggest downfall,' Sandy said to herself as she drove home.

Sandy thought about Ras; she had not heard from him for a few days, she knew that he was upset with her. Although she should not care, she felt guilty, the ending was not pleasant. The truth is she knew that he did not do anything wrong, and she did not mind him getting a drink. It was hard trying to have a life and do what she wanted to do whilst still raising her children and teaching them values and, at the same time, trying not to be a hypocrite. She knew Ras was a broke arse, but she still liked him, and she missed him. Sandy loved the way he touched her, how he held her, and made love. He knew how to position her, and how to stroke her pussy with his penis, just the thought of Ras made her wet. Sex with Ras was like crack, and she was the crackhead, she was addicted to his penis. Yet she knew that she had to let him go because the relationship was stagnated, and Sandy wanted more than occasional sex.

Chapter 7

Teddy arrived promptly at seven o'clock. Samuel and Scott were sitting in the kitchen; they had just finished eating their dinner of tuna and pasta with peppers and sweetcorn.

'Samuel, Scott, this is my friend Teddy,' said Sandy, standing next to Teddy, smiling.

Samuel and Scott stood up and looked at Teddy, scrutinising him. Teddy walked up to them and made a fist to spud them both.

'Rah, you two are tall,' said Teddy, looking up at the two of them. They both gave a little smile and spudded his fist. 'It's finally nice to meet you both, I know your mum long, time, yeh long time. I remember you two when you were both down here.' said Teddy, showing the hand measurement to his waist. 'Look at you both now, I can see that you both like to work out. That's good man keep it up, that was me in my younger days. Your mum told me that you have your own company,' said Teddy looking directly at Samuel.

'Yeh,' replied Samuel, nodding.

'And you're into games?'

'Yep, that's me, I love games,' replied Scott, standing with his arms folded looking down at Teddy.

'What do you do?' Samuel asked Teddy.

'Well, right now I'm trying to sort out tings but I'm looking to have my own business soon. I want to run my own wine bar/restaurant. I'd rather work for myself. I don't like working for people. No, I don't like it,' said Teddy, shaking his head.

'Yeh, it's good having your own business but it's hard work,' replied Samuel.

'Would you like a drink, Teddy?' interrupted Sandy.

'Babes, I'm okay right now, just trying to reason with your sons.'

'I know that having your own business is hard work but it's yours, you're not putting in all that work for someone else,' he said to them.

'Yeh, that's true,' replied Samuel.

'We need to leave, look at the time,' Scott said to Samuel.

'Where are you two off to?' asked Sandy.

'We're going to meet Nick,' replied Scott.

'Well, nice to meet you,' said Samuel, holding out his fist to spud Teddy. Teddy spudded them both as they were leaving.

'Tell your aunty that I will call her if you see her!' shouted Sandy to her sons.

'We're meeting Nick at the wine bar in Crystal Palace, we're not going to Aunty Jackie's house!'.

'Oh, okay then!'.

'Your sons seem nice, babes, yeh, nice. I can tell that they're protective over you though, very protective. I see them sizing me up, but it's all good though, it's all good. That's how it's supposed to be, babes, boys need to look after their mother.'

'Yes, they're protective. Can I get you a drink now?' asked Sandy.

'What you have?' replied Teddy whilst looking around the kitchen.

'I have juice or wine.'

'Wine, babes, wine, don't you have anything stronger like rum?'

'I have white rum,' replied Sandy.

'Rum, that sounds better. Yes, I have some rum with a little juice. I like your garden, it's nice and big, open the door let me check it out?'

Sandy opened the patio door and they both went into the garden. The garden was spacious, there was built up decking at the end of the garden where she had placed a wooden table with a large umbrella in the middle of the table and four wicker chairs. The rest of the garden was covered with grass.

'Babes how come you don't have no flowers or vegetables growing?' asked Teddy.

Sandy chuckled. 'I know, you're not the first person to ask me that question. I do plan to grow some, but the truth is I'm not green fingered, and nor are the children. Plus, I don't have the time to maintain it. I just about keep the grass trimmed.'

'Hi, mum,' said Cass, standing at the patio doors, smiling. Teddy turned around and looked towards her.

'Hi, honey,' replied Sandy smiling. 'Come meet my friend Teddy.' Cass walked up to Teddy and held out her hand.

'Hi,' said Cass.

'Hi, baby girl, nice to meet you,' replied Teddy whilst holding Cass's hand with both hands. 'This is one of the twins?' he asked.

'Yes,' replied Sandy.

'Well, nice to meet you, I'll leave you two alone, I've got homework,' said Cass as she released her hand and walked back into the house.

'Nice children, babes, nice children, they have manners, yes I like that, I like that. I need to introduce you to my children one day, they will like you.'

Sandy smiled. 'Let's go back inside it's a bit chilly out here,' she said.

'You have a nice big garden, nice and spacious. It would be good to do a barbecue when we get some summer,' said Teddy as they walked back to the house.

'I do barbecues sometimes,' replied Sandy, locking her patio doors.

'Where's your other daughter, the one I saw the other night?'

'Sophia, she's at home with her family.'

'No, not that one the younger one, the other twin.'

'Oh, Cammy, she's working late tonight.'

'What does she do?'

'She's a make-up artist. So, what are your plans for this evening?' asked Sandy, changing the conversation.

'My plans are with you babes; you know I like you and I know that it's important to you that I meet your children. I told you from the other day that I want to make love to you'.

Teddy pulled Sandy's chair towards him and sat on the edge of his chair so that her legs were between his legs. He ran his hands up and down her legs and looked in her eyes.

'Your skin is so soft, you feel so good, so good. I need you babes; I need to feel that fat pussy again.'

Sandy looked at Teddy and smiled as his stare penetrated her soul. She knew that she should tell him to go home but her pussy was too wet.

She wanted him as much as he wanted her. Sandy held his hand and led him up the stairs to her bedroom.

Sandy locked her bedroom door as Teddy walked into the bathroom. She drew her curtains and turned on her bedside lamp. She switched on her small music system and played her H-Town CD, 'Knocking Your Boots'. Sandy smiled and started to undress. She heard the shower running. 'Babes, you're feeling me, come join me!' shouted Teddy. Sandy smiled and climbed into the shower; the warm water ran along her body. Sandy looked into Teddy's eyes, they both stood still observing each other's body saying nothing with their mouths only with their eyes. Sandy loved how stiff and erect his penis was, she smiled and licked her lips. Teddy saw Sandy's reaction as she looked at his penis and smiled. He held his penis and stroked it back and forth. 'This is all for you, babes, all yours.' 'Sandy smiled and grasped his penis, stroking it back and forth. Teddy held Sandy's erect nipples between his fingers and started to kiss her deeply, rolling his tongue around her tongue and gently biting her lips. He softly kissed her neck, going along her body until his mouth reached her nipples. Teddy held her breasts and sucked them deeply whilst rubbing her clitoris with his finger. Sandy let out a deep moan. 'Fuck, babes, I'm going to explode!' exclaimed Teddy, breathing deeply. He turned her around, and lifted one of her legs, and thrust his penis into her vagina. Sandy left out a yelp and braced herself with her palms against the tiles.

'Your pussy is so fucking sweet, so fucking sweet. Oh God, this feels so good, aww yes babes,' said Teddy as he came inside her. 'Let's finish showering and get ready for round two.'

Sandy handed Teddy a towel from the small white wooden closet in her bathroom. Teddy watched Sandy as she dried herself.

'Lie down on the bed, let me lotion your body.'

Sandy handed Teddy the body lotion and lay on her bed as requested. Teddy took his time massaging Sandy's body. He rubbed her breasts then took his time rolling his finger on her erect nipples, twiddling them between his fingers. Sandy smiled and closed her eyes.

'You like that?'

'Very much, you're very good with your hands,' smiled Sandy.

'Do you have any olive oil?' asked Teddy.

'Yes, on the side in the bathroom.'

Teddy went into the bathroom to retrieve the olive oil. He then began to lotion her legs and motioned Sandy to open her legs further apart. He poured some of the olive oil onto the tip of his finger and began massaging Sandy's clitoris, then pushed his middle finger into her vagina, stroking it back and forth. Sandy relaxed her legs open.

'Aww, babes, oh shit,' responded Sandy.

'Just relax and close your eyes, I want to see you come.'

As Sandy started to pulsate. Teddy pushed his penis into her vagina and began thrusting back and forth. Sandy wanted to scream as she was orgasming. Teddy quickly covered her mouth with his mouth and began kissing her to muffle her scream. They both came together. Teddy rolled over and held her in his arms.

'Fuck, babes, you turn me on so much, so fucking much, you're mine babes, you're mine.' He kissed her forehead and yawned.

Sandy lay in his arms in deep thought, she did not know if she wanted to be with him. She was uncomfortable with him saying that she was all his. Sandy was afraid of commitment; she wanted a relationship but at the same time it scared her when someone wanted to get too close to her. Sandy knew where she stood with Ras. She knew that they would never have a committed relationship, so she could never be disappointed. Sandy wanted a trusting relationship and yet, whenever she came close to having one, she would somehow sabotage it. Sandy knew that she needed to settle down. She wanted to grow old with a man she could rely on who sincerely loved her. She was not sure that Teddy was that man.

There were a few things about Teddy that Sandy did not like. Sandy liked a man to have pride and she loved chivalry. She did not like the way Teddy had observed her house as if he wanted to move in, which would never be the case.

Sandy awoke to a rustling noise.

'I'm going, babes,' said Teddy.

'What time is it?' asked Sandy, adjusting her vision to see the time on her bedside clock.

'It's six o'clock, I'm leaving before your household wakes up. I'm busy today, go back to sleep babes, I'll call you later,' whispered Teddy.

Sandy checked her front door once he had left then went back to bed where she curled up and fell asleep.

Sandy was sitting in her lounge relaxing and watching the six o'clock news when Samuel walked in and sat next to her.

'Hi son, how was your day? You look tired.'

'I am tired,' replied Samuel, 'it was a long day.'

'I also feel a bit tired as I saw four clients today and one of the sessions was draining. Luckily, she was my last client.'

Samuel smiled and nodded his head in agreement.

'So, what do you think about my friend Teddy?'

'I think that you should keep him as a friend and nothing else,' replied Samuel whilst flicking through the TV channels.

Sandy looked at Samuel wide-eyed. 'Why do you say that?'

'Mum, this guy is in his 50s or thereabouts. If he has not made anything of his self yet he never will. At his age. mum, where is he going to get the money to open a business? No bank is going to lend him the money. Furthermore, does he have any skills? He's not even working, mum. The man is a waste of time, he's probably looking for you to secure a business for him. Mum, you need a man on your level, and neither he nor that using Ras is on your level.'

'I hear you,' replied Sandy, feeling quite embarrassed.

There was a pause. Sandy was surprised at Samuel's outburst as he did not usually make his feelings known.

'I'm hungry, what did you cook, mum?' asked Samuel, rubbing his stomach.

'Curry chicken and rice and you're lucky that I cooked; you know that I don't usually cook on a Friday,' replied Sandy.

'That's true, I forgot, thanks mum,' replied Samuel as he made his way to the kitchen.

Sandy knew that Samuel was right. She felt that Teddy had forced the idea of meeting her children, from the day he had pretended that he did not hear her outburst on the phone. She did not want Teddy to feel that now he had been to her house, he had got his foot under the table. Samuel had made a good point about Teddy's financial situation. The truth was she had never really paid him any mind, she had just let him talk because she had not taken him seriously. She knew that Samuel was right to disapprove of Teddy and she also knew that the rest of the children would feel the same.

'I should have stood my ground and not allowed him to take control and come to my house. He's not coming back,' Sandy thought to herself.

'Hi, mum,' said Cammy, interrupting Sandy's thoughts. You forgot your phone in the kitchen, it's been ringing off the hook. I think it's that crazy Teddy.'

'Most probably is,' replied Sandy.

'I heard that he was here yesterday, I don't know why you have to invite these crazy fools into our home, you need to keep your business to yourself mum.'

Sandy thought it best not to answer Cammy. She had heard enough from Samuel and Cammy was way too abrupt at times.

'So, how was work today?' Sandy asked, changing the subject.

'It was okay. Some of the customers can be a bit much sometimes. Some of them are so ugly and they think that make-up can work some form of miracle. Sometimes I want to tell them that make-up can only do so much. It's so hard to bite my tongue.'

'We all want beauty,' laughed Sandy.

'Anyway, got to get ready, I have a date tonight,' said Cammy, smiling.

'A date, that's nice, who's the lucky man?' asked Sandy.

'It's this guy I met a few weeks ago. We've been chatting on the phone quite a bit. I feel he's genuine. He's tall and hot.'

'So, what does he do?'

'He's an accountant,' replied Cammy, 'Which is good because I am rubbish at maths.'

'Okay, well enjoy.'

Sandy checked her phone as Cammy walked out of the lounge then went upstairs. She had two missed calls from Ras, one from Caroline, one from Joan, and 10 from Teddy. Just then, her phone began to ring again, it was Teddy.

'Hi, Teddy.'

'Hi Teddy, is that all you're saying? Do you know how long I have been ringing your phone? Just now you're answering. And before you make an excuse about work. I know that you don't work past four on a Friday, so what's your excuse this time?'

'Teddy first don't dictate the time I work until; I work for myself so if a client wants to see me past 4 p.m. then I will!' exclaimed Sandy, feeling quite agitated.

'So, did you work past four?'

'No, I did not Teddy! You're not the only person I have a miss call from. My phone is not pinned to me.'

'You know what, Sandy, I don't like the way you're talking to me. No, I don't like it, so I talk to you next time.'

Teddy hung up. Sandy looked at the phone and shook her head, she had enough of Teddy and did not care if she had offended him. Sandy did not like the way he continuously wanted to assert control over her. She called Caroline back.

'Hi, honey, sorry I missed your call.'

'It's okay.' replied Caroline. 'Have you heard from Joan yet?'

'I missed a call from her, and I have not spoken with her yet. Why, is everything okay?' asked Sandy.

'Don't tell me that you forgot that it's our girls' night out this evening?'

'Oh, shit, you're right, too much crap on my mind, Caroline. So, where are we going?'

'That cocktail bar on Lancaster street, Amora, the one that Joan picked,' replied Caroline. 'This is not like you Sandy, you're always on point. You need this girls' night out to clear your head of foolishness.'

'That's true', laughed Sandy. 'I know the place.'

'We're meeting up for 8 p.m.'

'Yes, sounds good, see you in a bit,' replied Sandy.

Sandy was glad to get out of her house, she needed a drink. She felt like the child in her own home and she had enough of the men in her life and the silly choices that she makes. She just needed a different environment and adults that were not her children to speak to. She quickly got ready and left the house.

Chapter 8

Sandy saw Caroline parking her car just as she pulled up on Lancaster Street. 'Good timing,' Sandy said to Caroline, smiling as she walked up to her.

'A bit chilly tonight,' said Caroline as she adjusted her black leather jacket.

They both walked into the wine bar and found a small table near the far end of the bar. Jazz music was playing in the background. The lighting was dim. The atmosphere was relaxing. As they both sat at their table, Joan walked in looking around. Sandy waved her hand.

'Hi, ladies!' shouted Joan, waving back as she strutted across the floor towards them. Joan was of medium height and had a light brown complexion. She was plump and round and very shapely. She has two children, a boy called Jamie, age 16, and a girl named Naomi, age 14.

Joan is very loud and flamboyant and says whatever came to her mind without any care. Her hair was naturally curly which she exaggerated with curly extensions to give a fuller look. She is very attractive, and she knows how to dress. She wore black skinny jeans with a yellow blouse, black high heeled knee-high boots, and a black fur jacket.

'Wow, this place is quite dark, I could hardly see where I was going,' she said as she pulled out a chair to sit down.

'Well, you chose it,' replied Caroline.

'Yes, I know,' responded Joan as she looked around the bar. 'It's quite nice here though, it would be romantic with a date. A little feel up under the table, no one would see,' she laughed as she picked up the drinks menu. 'So, anything new ladies, no-one found a husband yet?'

'This husband lark is harder than I thought,' responded Sandy.

'Even when you have the man, it's still hard to get him to ask you to marry him, and I will not ask him,' interrupted Caroline.

'You need to try subtle hints,' said Sandy.

'Subtle hints do not work with this man, you will need a bull-dozer and even then, he may not get it.' Joan and Sandy both laughed. 'His motto is if it's not broken don't try to fix it, let it be.'

'Then lock down the pussy from him, that's more than a subtle hint,' replied Joan.

'I may just do that,' laughed Caroline. Is it really that hard to get engaged, ladies?'

'Are you ready to order, ladies?' interrupted the waitress.

'What are you having girls?' Caroline asked.

'I'll have a Long Island Iced Tea,' Sandy responded.

'I'll have a Porn Star Martini,' said Caroline.

'So, will I,' said Joan.

'It is hard if you want to be with the right man,' said Sandy, continuing the conversation. 'These men nowadays want the woman to be the man. I've been thinking about life, and I feel drained from trying.'

'That's because you're trying with the wrong sort of men in the first place,' Caroline responded.

'Listen to her,' interrupted Joan. 'Once you meet a man and he does not have a J O B, why are you even entertaining him? It's gone bad before it even starts.'

'Mm, mm,' responded Caroline, nodding her head.

'You're both right, it's true. I'm just not sure that I am interested in finding a husband or getting engaged yet. I need some time to myself to think things through. I mean, why do you both want to get married?' asked Sandy.

'I know that something has happened for this change of thought, what's going on?' asked Caroline.

Sandy took a deep breath and shook her head. 'I don't even know where to start.'

'Just jump in and start wherever,' laughed Caroline.

'Well, Teddy stayed over last night. He came early enough to meet the children which I suppose he thought gave him the go-ahead to start staying over.'

'Okay, okay, rewind,' interrupted Caroline. 'I know I said start wherever, but this is too far forward. When did he start going to your house and, more importantly, why?' Caroline stared at Sandy, waiting for an answer.

'Don't look at me like that, Caroline.'

'Like what?'

'Like a strict parent.'

'You both need to hold up because I'm lost here. Who the hell is Teddy?' asked Joan. Sandy and Caroline laughed.

'I'll give you a quick synopsis, 'laughed Sandy.

'No, I'll give her the synopsis,' interrupted Caroline. 'Your synopsis will take all evening'. Sandy rolled her eyes. 'Well,' continued Caroline, 'we all know how broke and shit Ras is?'

'Um, um, sorry. Sandy, but it's true,' Joan nodded.

'So, my dear lovely lady here decided to date an old friend. He has a lot of children and baby mamas and is also an ex-offender. In her strange processing mind, she thought that he was better than Ras. He calls her phone every minute, which in my opinion is a sign of possessiveness, and now, basically, he has been to her house, met her kids and she's sleeping with him. So that's it in a nutshell,' Caroline finished.

'Waitress! Can we have the same again, please?' shouted Joan across the bar, as she quickly backed her drink. 'Sorry ladies, but I need a next drink. I'm sure you both do too, otherwise I will drink yours for you. Sandy, you know I love you to bits,' Joan continued, 'but girl, this is some foolishness here. What's going on in your head?'.

'Thanks, Caroline, for your so-call synopsis, which I am not happy with,' snapped Sandy.

'So, what have I said that was wrong?'

'It's not about what you said, it's the way you said it. Yes, obviously, it sounds bad but there's a lot more to it,' responded Sandy.

'I tell you what more there is to it, your pussy twitch too much,' laughed Joan.

'Yes, that too,' laughed Sandy.

'Okay, now I know the gist of it, continue with the story,' said Joan.

'Well, we went out on Friday to the Culture Club and then had sex after the club. He left early Saturday morning, but he was ringing my phone as he does within a couple of hours after he had left. I missed the call and when I did answer, he wanted to know why I had not answered my phone from the first ring. Then that same evening, he wanted to come to my house after a dance at 4 a.m. Basically, I got pissed off and told him that my children did not know him and I was not going to answer my door at that time of the morning. '

'Hold up,' Caroline interrupted, raising her hand to halt the conversation. 'There's something missing here, go a bit slower. Did he ask you to go to the party with him?'

'No,' replied Sandy, shaking her head.

'Okay, cheeky little shit, so when you told him that your children did not know him, what did he say?' asked Caroline.

'That's the thing. He did not answer me. I knew that he was still on the phone because I heard the traffic in the background. But he pretended as if he had hung up the phone, which I found quite unnerving. I had not heard from him for days. Then yesterday, he's ringing me wanting to come around and meet the children. When I reminded him about his silence on the phone, he acted as if he was oblivious to what I was talking about.'

'Sandy, I don't know this man, but I do not like him; I'm going to tell you something as a friend and someone who loves you dearly. You need to be careful of this man, he's calculating, conniving, possessive, controlling, and damn right rude. Firstly, he wants to turn up at your door at 4 a.m. He has not asked you if you want to go out with him but when he finishes partying then he wants to go to your house to sleep.'

Caroline backed the prosecco shot and shook her head. 'He is full of shit but, Sandy, it's your fault, you let him in too quick.'

'Furthermore,' Joan interrupted, 'if you wanted a fuck then you should have gone back to his place.'

'Joan's right because he should not have been at your house yesterday either. You're too soft sometimes, Sandy, and he knows it. Anyway, let me finish what I'm saying now because you told the awful shit that your children did not know him, and he says nothing and pretends that he did not hear you. Then, decides to get around you by saying that he wants to meet your children. Sandy, you know that I don't like to swear. May the Lord forgive me, but you should have told him to fuck off and jump in a stream and float away.'

'Wow,' chuckled Sandy, shaking her head, 'I have not seen you this angry for a long time, Caroline.'

'Because he's a liberty taker, Sandy, and he has an agenda. Please don't let him back into your house,' said Caroline.

'I can't; Samuel and Cammy already gave me a mouthful.'

'You see the foolishness, Sandy. You have done a lot for your children, and they look up to you, don't let these arsehole men interrupt that. Ras and now this one don't have any good intention for you or your children, it's all about them, Sandy. Plus, this love of sex is going to get you into trouble. Sandy, get a damn vibrator,' responded Caroline.

'I don't know about this vibrator thing. I don't like to fuck myself, nor does Sandy, Caroline, otherwise she would not be in this predicament. So, Sandy who fucks better? Ras or this new one?' Joan asked, laughing.

Sandy laughed. 'No one can fuck or sweet me like Ras. You're right he is so full of shit, but he can fuck. Teddy ain't saying nothing, so I can easily let him go. Plus, I need some time out to focus on myself. So, what's going on with you, Joan?' asked Sandy.

'I'm still seeing Marcus; he gives me money and buys me anything I want and sucks my pussy damn good. Just thinking about it now is making me wet,' laughed Joan whilst adjusting herself in her seat.

'I swear you're too much, Joan, sometimes. So, do you think that marriage may be on the table?' asked Sandy.

'Are you telling me that out of the two men that you're fucking, Sandy, none of them suck your pussy?' Sandy opened her eyes.

'My dear girl, I am not sleeping with two men as I no longer sleep with Ras, and no, none of them suck my vagina and yes, I am okay with that,' responded Sandy with a slight grin.

'Please, girl, don't even try this posh shit with me as if your shit don't stink. I'm sure that you only stopped fucking Ras about a week or two ago,' replied Joan.

'Good luck to you taking her on as if you don't know how raw she is,' laughed Caroline.

'So,' Sandy continued, 'is marriage on the cards or not?'

'Maybe, he has not asked yet but he's always around me and the children. He does whatever I ask of him.'

'Do the children like him?' asked Caroline.

'They better fucking like him,' responded Joan, 'he spends a lot of money on them as well. Plus, he gives them pocket money, which is more than their so-called dad has done in years. They do like him though; they get on very well. He wants to take us all to Disneyland Florida in the summer holidays.'

'Um, did you hear that, Sandy? Disneyland Florida after spending so much money on Joan and the children and there's you telling me that I have enough money to pay for myself'.

'Sandy, you really said that Caroline should pay for herself. So, what is the point of her having a man if he cannot take her and her children on holiday?' asked Joan.

'Exactly!' responded Caroline, looking at Sandy.

'What the fuck? Is this pick on Sandy day today?'

Caroline and Joan both laughed.

'All I was saying is that whether he pays for the holiday or not, Caroline can more than afford it herself.'

'Sandy, this is your problem and why broke men gravitate to you. Because if you don't want to spend their money, they will spend yours. Play fucking broke, even when you have, you don't have. You're a single woman and you need help. In the bible, it says ask and you shall receive, so start asking,' said Joan.

'Amen to that,' responded Caroline, clapping her hands.

Chapter 9

Sandy had been ignoring both Teddy's and Ras's calls for the past week. She had received at least a hundred missed calls from Teddy. Sandy hoped that he would realise that she was not answering his calls because her interest in a relationship with him had waned and the phone calls would end. Sandy missed Ras as they had not spoken to each other for about three weeks. Sandy knew that if she spoke to Ras, things between them would start all over again. It was best to leave it alone and hope that he had also got the message that their so-called relationship had ended. Sandy feared Teddy most of all because she knew that he was unpredictable and did not want him to turn up at her house. She told the children that if either of them came to the door to say that she was out, which they were more than happy to do.

Sandy thought about Shaun whom she had met two weeks ago in Café Nero; he was different from Ras and Teddy. She liked that he worked, she especially liked that he worked in construction. Sandy preferred men that worked with their hands and did a hard day's work. Sandy liked his dimples and thought that he was quite good looking. She also liked his mannerisms and politeness. Sandy decided to call him, hoping that he would remember her.

The phone rang, Sandy felt nervous and thought of hanging up then she heard,

'Hi,' in a deep voice.

'Hi Shaun, this is Sandy, I, um met you in the coffee shop. I mean Café Nero a couple of weeks ago. I don't know if...'

'Hi Sandy,' interrupted Shaun, 'of course, I remember you. How could I forget such a pretty face?'

Sandy laughed. 'I'm sorry that it took me so long to ring you, I've just been really busy.'

'It's okay, Sandy, I do understand, life gets like that sometimes. I'm just happy to finally hear from you. You've caught me at a good time as I've not too long reached home from work. Finished a little earlier than usual today.'

Sandy looked at the time and realised that it was 5.30 p.m.

'So, what time do you usually finish work?' she asked.

'I work from 8 'til 5 but today I finished at 4. Been working a bit of overtime because we want to get the project finished and move on to a new one.'

'You've got a nice boss, sometimes these bosses don't care how much they work their employees.'

'That's true,' laughed Shaun, 'Lucky for me, I'm the boss or, I should say, my dad and I own the company.' Sandy raised her eyebrows and smiled. 'It's nice when families go into business together. So, what made you both decide on construction?'

'Well, my dad's a builder by trade and I'm a qualified plumber. Once you're in this industry you meet a lot of people who are qualified in one thing or another, so it makes it easier to find skilled people. Plus, a lot of these companies don't like to pay properly, it's better to have your own business.'

'I totally agree with you, which is why I also work for myself.'

'You work for yourself, I'm impressed, so where are you based?' he asked.

'I work from home, It's a lot easier, no overheads, etc.'

'Yeh, I hear you. So now that I have finally heard from you, could I take you out for dinner sometime soon?'

'Yes, nice of you to ask,' replied Sandy.

'How about this Saturday if that's okay with you?' asked Shaun.

Sandy thought for a moment, trying to think if she had any plans for this weekend.

'This Saturday is fine.'

'So, what sort of food do you like?' he asked.

'I like Chinese, Italian, Thai, or Caribbean,' She replied.

'That's great. I also like Thai, there is a great Thai restaurant in West London. I know the owner. I did some work on his shop for him. I will book the table for 8 p.m. if that's okay with you?'

'8 is okay.'

'I can pick you up if you don't mind.'

Sandy was not ready to let Shaun know where she lived, she wanted to take her time and get to know him.

'That's nice of you but I will meet you on Headcorn Road, Thornton Heath, and jump in your car.'

'Yes, that's okay, I know the road. It will be nice to see you again. I still remember that pretty smile,' said Shaun.

Sandy smiled.

'Yes, see you on Saturday or should I say tomorrow?' he said.

'See you tomorrow, Shaun,' replied Sandy, feeling nervous and excited as she hung up the phone.

'Mum! You need to come to the door!' shouted Cammy from downstairs.

'Who's at the door?' asked Sandy, feeling confused as she did not expect any visitors.

'You need to come down mum!'

'I'm coming!'

Sandy jumped off her bed and slipped her feet into her fluffy pink slippers and hurried down the stairs to see who was at the front door. Cammy stood at the door and looked up at Sandy then she shook her head and stepped away from the door, so Sandy could take her place. The expression on Cammy's face gave Sandy a lump in her throat. She knew it was either Ras or Teddy, she did not want a confrontation with either of them. Her jaw almost hit the ground when she saw Ras standing at the door and Teddy leaning against the wall of her driveway. Sandy froze and felt hot sweat all over her body; she wanted to shut her front door and run at the same time as wishing she could disappear. Sandy did not know what to do or what to say. Cammy stood behind her mum, which helped Sandy to feel a little less nervous because she knew she was not on her own.

'I have not heard from you for weeks. What happened. you meet a new man?' asked Ras, giving Sandy a piercing look.

Sandy knew that Ras was angry; the last time they had spoken he had been upset with her. This was a normal time distance between the two of them, on and off all the time. She knew that she and Ras always made it up until the next argument. This time was different as Ras has never seen another man around Sandy. She could feel his anger. Sandy would have cussed and shut her door if it had been just Ras. She knew that although she had ignored both their phone calls, she had not officially broken it off with either of them. Although Teddy was standing a small distance away, she could see that he was observing her and listening for her reply. She knew that they were both unpredictable and she did not want any embarrassment at her front door. Sandy looked at both men and opened her mouth to speak but nothing would come out.

'Answer the man, let him know that you have a new man!' shouted Teddy. Ras turned and looked at Teddy.

Sandy's eyes darted between the two men. Her legs felt weak, and her heart was beating fast.

'Pussy-hole who you talking to? Move yourself from here! Sandy, tell this man who I am. It's obvious that this fool doesn't know who I am, or he would not even start to chat to me!' shouted Ras.

Sandy could not speak, she felt numb.

'Get the fuck from my woman's door, pussy!' shouted Teddy, walking up to Ras.

Ras turned around to face Teddy, his fists clenched. Sandy had never seen Ras this angry, and she began to tremble. Everything started to move in slow motion, Sandy froze.

Scott and Samuel both barged Sandy out the way and ran out the front door.

'Yo, yo, yo!' they shouted, placing themselves in between Ras and Teddy. 'You can't start no war around here, not on our doorstep!' shouted Samuel.

Ras and Teddy stopped in their tracks, still staring at each other.

'Look, you both have to sort this out individually at a different time with mum. Now is not the right time,' said Samuel, looking at both men.

Sandy knew that she had to be straight and honest - it was now or never. Sandy walked out into her driveway.

'Go back inside mum, we've got this,' said Scott.

'No, I need to be straight with you both.'

Both men looked at Sandy.

'I have not been returning either of your calls because I don't want to be with either of you.'

'Sandy you're so full of fucking shit! Why not just tell me that instead of ignoring my calls? You know what Sandy, don't even answer, fuck you!' shouted Teddy.

Teddy turned around and walked off. Ras stared at Sandy.

'Don't stare at me like that, Ras.'

Samuel and Scott stepped aside, giving Sandy and Ras some space to speak.

'Sandy, I know that I fuck up a lot, but can we go inside and talk please?'

Sandy could see her adults looking at her and she knew what their look meant.

'No, Ras, enough is enough, I just want to be on my own.'

'On your own. If you wanted to be on your own, a next man would have not been here.'

Sandy stared at him, she could see the hurt, she felt tears coming to her eyes.

'Look after yourself, babes,' said Sandy, as she walked away and went inside her house.

She could feel Ras's eyes burning into her back, but she did not turn around. Sandy went upstairs to her bedroom. She curled up on her bed and cried, the tears flowing. Sandy hugged her pillow and covered her mouth to muffle her crying.

The following morning, Sandy awoke with the rays of the sun gleaming through her window. She looked at her bedside clock and saw it was 6 a.m. Sandy realised that she had cried herself to sleep and had not moved from yesterday evening. She had not closed her curtains and they were still wide open. Sandy went to the bathroom, used the toilet, and washed her face, then lay back on her bed thinking of the day before. She could see the whole scene playing out in her mind like a slow-motion movie. Ras at the front door and Teddy standing in the back looking at her. Her stomach churned when she remembered the look in their eyes. 'My worst nightmare came alive,' she thought to herself, 'So embarrassing in front of the children. None of them have even bothered to check on me. I wonder if the neighbours saw anything.'

She could still see the hurt in Ras's eyes and tears started to flow again. She knew that this was the end, there was no turning back. Although she wanted it to end, this was not the way. Her stomach churned and she felt sick. Sandy looked at her clock and realised that it was 8 a.m., two hours had passed so quickly. She went downstairs to make herself a hot drink and toast.

Sandy sat at the kitchen table, holding her cup of nettle tea staring into space.

'Morning mum, mum, mum!' shouted Cammy.

Sandy jumped; Cammy had startled her.

'You okay, mum, you know how long I've been calling you?'

'Oh, sorry Cammy, I did not hear you.'

'You should be happy mum, you run the damn fool man dem.'

'Yeh, you're right, Cammy. I'm surprised that I slept for so long. None of you came to check on me. My curtains were wide open when I awoke.'

'I did look in, but you were fast asleep. I heard you crying earlier so I left you alone to do your thing. If you're in the house I know that you're okay, mum. The truth is mum. I don't even know why you were crying,' Cammy continued, 'It's not as if you saw any of them all the time plus they're broke arse men, mum'.

Sandy sipped her tea and said nothing. She knew that it was pointless to explain anything to Cammy as she did not like either of them, especially Ras.

'Wow, mum, I heard about the commotion yesterday. Lucky your big sons were around or there would have been war on our doorstep. You're lucky that men want to fight over you at your age,' laughed Cassandra, as she walked into the kitchen. 'Anyway, good riddance to bad rubbish. So, what're your plans for today, mum? Should we go out and celebrate tonight?'

Sandy shook her head. 'You girls are really something else, actually, I have a date tonight,' she said.

'A date! You move quick, mum!' exclaimed Cassandra.

'I hope that he is no broke arse man, mum, so who is he?' asked Cammy.

Sandy rolled her eyes. 'His name is Shaun and I met him a few weeks ago. He owns his own building business with his dad. He seems okay.'

'Sounds better already. I'm out of here before I'm late for work, bye mum.' said Cammy as she walked out of the kitchen.

'How come you're up so early?' Sandy asked Cassandra.

'Still working on this damn dissertation. I can't wait until it's finished. So, mum,' Cassandra continued, 'what's going on with you?'

'What do you mean?'

'Well, mum, what happened yesterday, now you're going on a date tonight. I'm just wondering if you're okay. I know that we did not like Ras, but I know that you liked him.'

'That's life, Cassandra, sometimes liking someone is not enough. Although I do take responsibility for yesterday's embarrassing incident,' said Sandy, lowering her head and staring at her cup of tea. She took a deep breath and continued, 'I should have told them both that it was over rather than ignoring their calls. I never expected them both to turn up at my door. Uh, so damn embarrassing.'

'Mum it's not as bad as you think, forget it.'

'Um, it will take some time to forget, Cass.'

'So, who is this Shaun guy?' Cassandra asked, sitting down at the table next to Sandy with her cup of coffee and two slices of toast with strawberry jam. Sandy smiled.

'I met Shaun a few weeks ago in a coffee shop after supervision. I only called him yesterday, just before all that commotion.'

'You don't seem very excited about seeing him. You have not even spoken about him or anything, that's not like you mum, you're usually more excited.'

'Yeh, true, I've been thinking about life a lot more, I guess. I want a good man in my life, so I need to make better choices,' replied Sandy.

'So where are you and Shaun going this evening?' Cassandra asked.

'We're going to a Thai restaurant in West London.'

'Thai, I love Thai food!' exclaimed Cassandra. 'Sounds nice. Well, have fun, mum. I'm going back to my room to continue with this dissertation,' said Cassandra, rolling her eyes.

Sandy smiled. 'It will all be over soon, honey.'

Sandy went upstairs to her bedroom and laid on her bed, looking up at the ceiling. She laughed as she thought about what Caroline and Joan would both make of the situation. Sandy's thoughts were disturbed by her phone. She decided to ignore it, then it rang again straight away. She picked it up and realised that Teddy was ringing her. Sandy felt nervous and fearful at the same time. She did not want to answer the phone, but she did not want Teddy to turn up at her door again either. Looking at her phone, she saw 13 missed calls, Sandy felt a knot in her stomach. She took a deep breath.

'Hi Teddy', said Sandy. There was no answer, Sandy said nothing, she could hear the faint sound of music in the background.

'Sandy, Sandy,' said Teddy.

'Hi.'

'Is that all you got to fucking say, Sandy, hi?'

Sandy was scared and wanted to hang up the phone. She knew that Teddy was angry with her and did not want to upset him any further than she had already done.

'I'm sorry about everything that happened yesterday Teddy, I really am I should have...'

'You're, sorry, you're sorry,' interrupted Teddy, 'You're fuckeries, Sandy! I thought you were better than that. So, tell me something, Sandy, were you fucking both of us at the same time?'

'No Teddy, I was not.'

'Don't fucking lie to me Sandy, tell me the truth!'

Sandy started to shake, and tears came to her eyes.

'It's not like that, Teddy. I was seeing Ras before you and stopped when I started to see you.'

'So, if you stopped why was he at your door yesterday?'

Sandy shook her head; she did not know how to explain it all to Teddy.

'He wanted to get back with me and kept calling my phone, but I was ignoring his calls.'

'Just like you were ignoring mine?'

Sandy paused, she wanted to create a story, but she knew it was best to be honest.

'Yes,' replied Sandy.

'So, if you knew that you no longer wanted me, why just not tell me?'

'I don't know, Teddy, I'm sorry I should have been straight with both of you.'

'Don't fucking tell me about no next man, Sandy. I don't fucking care about no next man, I care about me! You know what, Sandy, I opened up to you Sandy, I opened up to you. I was honest about my past and situation, honest Sandy, honest!'

'I know, Teddy, I'm...'

'Don't fucking interrupt me, Sandy. I called you, you did not call me, so let me finish saying what I have to say.'

Tears were rolling down Sandy's cheeks.

'Sorry,' she said, sniffing and wiping her tears.

'Don't even bother with the tears, Sandy. You're the one who hurt me, not the other way around! It's not all about you, I have feelings too, feelings Sandy, feelings. That's the thing with you fucking women, you think that it's all about you and man don't have no feelings. Well, I have feelings, Sandy, believe it or not, yes me, Teddy who went to prison has feelings too. You know what the sad thing is, Sandy, I really liked you, really, really liked you. It's just hard to adjust when you come out of prison. I did not want to rely on you, I'm not that kind of man. I had a lot of things to sort out and I did not want to burden you with my problems. I'm a man Sandy, I'm a man and I needed time to sort myself out. You just needed to have some patience with me, patience Sandy, patience. So, tell me Sandy, have you met someone else?'

Sandy paused and thought about his question.

'So, have you fucking met someone Sandy?'

'No, I have not met anyone, Teddy,' replied Sandy.

Sandy knew that with Teddy's temperament, it was best not to mention Shaun. Moreover, she had not even been on a date with Shaun yet so technically, she was not lying.

'So why did you take so long to answer me then? Like you had to think about your answer?'

'Teddy, I'm tired and I'm sorry how things turned out, but I'm going now so take care of yourself, Teddy.'

'Fuck you, Sandy!' replied Teddy and he hung up the phone.

Sandy took a deep breath and sighed. She laid back on her bed and looked up at the ceiling. 'Such is fucking life,' she said to herself.

Chapter 10

Y ou look, nice, mum, where you off too?'
asked Cass, standing at Sandy's bedroom
doorway.

'I'm going on a date with that Shaun guy I was
telling you about.'

Sandy was standing in front of her mirror
fiddling with her earring. She wore red tailored
trousers with a black v- necked bodysuit and a
red bolero jacket. With open toe black heeled
sandals and a matching red necklace and
earrings, she completed her outfit with a black
clutch bag.

'Oh, yes. I forgot, mum - this dissertation takes
over my life so that I can hardly remember
anything else,' replied Cass as she walked into
Sandy's room and sat on her bed.

'I surely remember those days like a bad
toothache. I don't envy you, young lady, but it's
worth it, it's all worth it in the end.'

'On another note, mum, I err heard you on the
phone earlier. Mum, don't let anyone upset you.'

Sandy sat down on her bed next to Cass. She held her hand and rested her head on Cass's head.

'I'm okay babes, this is part and parcel of the breaking up. Sometimes smooth, sometimes a bit rough, it all blows over in time.'

'Was it Teddy on the phone?'

Sandy sighed, then sat up and nodded her head.

'He just needed to get what he felt off his chest. Life is strange, Cassandra, sometimes people care a lot more than you think they do.'

Cass hugged Sandy.

'Thanks, Cass, anyway that's the past and I have a date,' she said, standing up and smiling. 'I need to get going, I don't want to be late.'

'You look nice, mum, well-coordinated, have fun.'

Sandy hugged her daughter again. 'Love you, honey, and thanks for caring.'

Sandy pulled up on Headcorn street and parked. She realised that she did not know what type of car Shaun drove, so she was unsure whether he had arrived or not. Sandy pulled down her sun visor to look in the mirror. She smiled and was checking that her lipstick was okay and that there was no lipstick smudged on her teeth when she heard a knock on her car window. Sandy was startled, she quickly turned around and saw a man standing at her car door. Her heart raced; it took Sandy a moment to realise that it was Shaun. She felt both panic and embarrassment. Sandy turned off her engine and unlocked her car door. She grabbed her clutch bag and was ready to exit. Shaun smiled and opened her car door. He took her hand to assist her in getting out of the car.

'I'm sorry that I frightened you,' said Shaun with a big smile.

Sandy looked at him, admiring his lovely white teeth and dimples. She smiled.

'Thank you,' she said as she held his hand and stood up, 'I was surprised to see you, you recognised me and my car.'

'I apologise, I came 15 minutes earlier so that I would see when you arrived. I realised that we did not know what car each other drove.'

Shaun was parked a few cars behind Sandy, and he gestured in the direction towards where his car was parked. He walked a few steps ahead and opened the car door for Sandy. He drove a 16-plate navy blue Mercedes Benz, with grey leather interior.

'Thank you,' said Sandy as she sat down, grateful to be a passenger for once. Sandy liked the smell of the car. She could see and smell that it had recently been cleaned and polished.

'So, what music would you like to listen to?' asked Shaun as he sat in the car and started the engine. Keith Sweat singing 'Make It Last Forever' was playing.

'This is a nice song, although I do prefer 'Twisted'.'

'That's one of my favourites as well. A woman who knows her music, I like that. You look really nice, Sandy, lady in red.' Shaun looked at Sandy and smiled.

'Thank you, I do try. You look really smart as well, your dress code matches your car.'

Shaun laughed. 'This is purely coincidental, but yes, I do like blue as you can see. I supposed you like red?'

'Yes, I do, red is one of my favourite colours,' replied Sandy.

Shaun wore a navy-blue tailored suit with a blue and grey tee- shirt and black suede Clark shoes.

'It's nice to finally meet up with you, Sandy, I thought that I was never going to hear from you.'

Sandy looked at Shaun and smiled. Shaun relaxed backed in the car whilst driving, he looked comfortable and in control.

'I shouldn't tell you this, but I went to Café Nero every day since I met you, hoping to bump into you.' Shaun looked at Sandy and smiled as he pulled up to a traffic light.

'I only go there once a month after supervision, so I'm not due there for another two weeks.'

'That's right, you told me that the first time I met you, I totally forgot, well I'm glad that I don't have to wait another two weeks to see you,' Shaun chuckled.

Sandy observed Shaun's hands as he was driving; they looked thick and strong, and his nails were clean and neat as if he had a manicure. He wore a white gold ring encrusted with small diamonds on the middle finger of his left hand.

Shaun found a nice parking spot around the corner from the restaurant. 'Lucky that we found this parking spot, it's quite busy around here, especially on the weekends,' he commented.

'I'm not that familiar with this area, I only drive through it to get to wherever I'm going,' responded Sandy.

As Shaun opened his car door, Sandy followed suit. 'No, relax, I'll get your door,' Shaun insisted.

Sandy smiled as Shaun walked around the car and opened her door. He held out his hand and helped her out of the car.

'Thank you, Shaun, it's nice to see that chivalry has not died.'

Shaun smiled and held his arm out; Sandy held his arm as they walked to the restaurant.

The restaurant looked quite mediocre, not as flash as some she had seen; there were a couple of tables and chairs outside which were occupied.

Sandy thought that although it was late June, there was still a chill in the air. Shaun held the door open for Sandy. Inside, she observed the mirrors and the shimmering lights hanging over the mirrors. It was not as big as she had first anticipated but it was cosy.

'Hi Shaun, welcome, welcome, nice to see you, long time, long time,' said a small Asian man with a wide grin, holding out his hand to greet Shaun.

'Hi Michael, yes it has been a long time.' Shaun shook his hand and patted his shoulder. 'This is Sandy,' said Shaun as he turned around to introduce her.

'Hi Sandy,' said Michael as he held out his hand, 'Shaun don't come for long time, now he comes with pretty lady.'

Sandy smiled as she shook his hand.

'Come, come I have nice table waiting for you.' Sandy followed and Shaun pulled out the chair for her to sit down.

'Which wine do you like? Red or white? This one is on me. Shaun good man, he fix my shop,' said Michael.

'Which red wines do you have?' asked Sandy.

'Oh, she like red wine, Shaun also like red wine.'

Sandy looked at Shaun and smiled.

'We have Cabernet Sauvignon, Malbec, or Merlot,' said Michael.

'Which one do you like?' asked Sandy as she looked at Shaun.

'Don't worry about Shaun, you pick wine,' interrupted Michael.

Shaun laughed and smiled as he looked at Sandy.

'It's okay, I'm happy with anything that you choose,' replied Shaun.

'I'll have the Cabernet Sauvignon, thank you Michael,' said Sandy.

'So, what do you think of this place?' asked Shaun.

Sandy looked around. 'I like the gold trimmings on the wall and the spotlights on the ceiling, although it's quite dim. It's not extravagant but it's cosy, plus Michael is warm and friendly,' responded Sandy.

'Sometimes a place may be big and expensively decorated but the staff are not that nice, and the food is not that good either. It's better to have a cosy little place with good food and friendly staff.'

Sandy nodded in agreement.

Shaun opened his menu. 'So, what would you like to grace your palate with?'

Sandy smiled and looked at her menu.

'Which starter would you like?' asked Shaun.

'I'll have the vegetable tempura in batter and for the main, I'll have the pla rad prik in the batter. The trout instead of the cod,' Sandy replied.

'Don't you eat meat?' he asked, curious about Sandy's preference.

'No, I'm pescatarian,' replied Sandy.

Michael came back with the wine and poured them each a glass.

'Have you decided what you like to eat?'

Sandy told Michael her order. Shaun decided on prawn tempura in batter for his starter and ped ta krai for his main.

'The duck looks tempting, I used to like duck plus it goes down well with red wine,' said Sandy.

Shaun smiled. 'Yes, duck is one of my favourite meats. I thought you would have ordered the prawns or don't pescatarians eat prawns?'

Sandy laughed. 'Pescatarians can eat prawns, I just preferred something different today.'

'So, what made you decide to be vegetarian, I mean pescatarian, and what's the difference?'

'It just means that I eat fish and not just vegetables, although sometimes I can stick to veg. I decided not to eat meat because of the way meat is treated and what they feed the animals.'

'So, are your children also pescatarians?'

'No just myself, they like their meat, so I cook it for them.'

Shaun sat back in his chair and gave Sandy a strange look.

'Why the confused look?' she asked.

'I just find it strange that you feel that something is wrong with meat so you don't eat it and yet you will feed it to your children.'

Sandy raised her eyebrows and shifted in her seat.

'No, I'm not judging you or anything, I just find it a bit strange,' he said.

'It's a fair question,' responded Sandy, 'Although, I have children they are adults. I will not force my opinions on them. They feel that everything is bad, even the veg, they also feel that fish is no better than meat. I respect their decision and I leave it there. If anyone feels like changing their mind about what they choose to eat, the choice is theirs to make,' replied Sandy.

Shaun smiled. 'I like your answer, it makes sense. 'It is best to let people form their own understanding as to why they do or don't do something and that way, they will stick to whatever they're doing. Well, at least sometimes anyway.

Sandy laughed. 'So true, Shaun, I agree with you.'

Michael brought their meals to the table.

'This looks very nice,' said Sandy, looking at her dish and smiling.

'Also taste very good,' responded Michael, offering them more wine.

'Yes please, thank you,' Sandy replied.

Michael filled both their glasses.

Shaun nodded his head and smiled.

'This is nice, and I love the sauce,' she said, tasting her food.

'Yes, it is,' replied Shaun in agreement 'I forgot how nice his food is. Now that I've met you, Sandy, maybe we can come here again soon if you would like to?'

Shaun looked at Sandy, staring into her eyes. Sandy felt his penetrative stare that went right through her body straight to her vagina. She looked at him and smiled in return.

'Maybe, anything is possible,' replied Sandy.

'I like that,' laughed Shaun. 'So, tell me, Sandy, why is a lovely intelligent woman like yourself still single?'

'Well, I can ask the same about you, Shaun, why is a handsome, well-rounded man like yourself still single?'

Shaun stared at Sandy with a straight face.

'Because you're not in my life, Sandy.'

Sandy felt hot and blushed, not knowing where to look. Shaun then reached across the table and held her hand, continuing to stare into her eyes.

'I'm serious, Sandy, I would like to get to know you more, will you give me the chance to get close to you, let us start to get to know each other?'

Sandy felt her vagina pulsate. Fucking him was not a problem, he was built and handsome and made her tingle, but she was not sure about the relationship part. A part of her wanted a serious man in her life, and the little that she had seen of Shaun felt like husband material. She knew that he was worth getting to know, and her children and friends would like him. Yet, she was in two minds. Sandy found it hard to trust and she feared getting close to anyone and being hurt.

'What's wrong, Sandy, am I moving too quickly?'

'No, no,' responded Sandy with a smile, trying to change the mood and take away the seriousness of the conversation. 'It's just that I like to take my time. I do like you as a person, and I am open to getting to know you more.'

'I do understand, Sandy, sorry if I made you feel that I wanted to rush things. I just did not want this to be our last date. I was really happy when you called. I was wondering all sorts of things when I did not hear from you. Like if you had lost my number, or if I would ever see you again.'

Sandy laughed, moving her hand away from Shaun and taking a sip of her wine.

'Sorry I took some time to call you, I just had a lot of things to sort out. So, Shaun how long have you been single?'

'You like the food?' interrupted Michael.

'Yes, very nice as usual Michael, I can see that you have not lost your touch,' replied Shaun.

'Michael don't lose touch, food is always good,' said Michael, removing the dinner plates.

'It was very nice, thank you,' said Sandy.

'Yes, very nice, you see, Shaun, your lady enjoy my food, so you have to come more often,' laughed Michael. 'You choose dessert for me.'

'I'll have the mango sorbet, please,' answered Sandy.

'I'll have the same too, please,' Shaun responded.

'Okay, two mango sorbets coming up,' said Michael as he walked back to the kitchen.

'So, where were we?' said Shaun as he sipped his glass of wine and stared at Sandy.

'Well, I was asking you how long you have been single?'

'Oh yes, I forgot, I guess that I walked right into that one.' Shaun then leaned forward in his chair and looked at Sandy. 'To be straight with you, Sandy, I always wonder why women ask that question. I mean, why does it matter? I am single because I'm not in a relationship. I know that I like you and would like to get to know you better in hope that I can have a serious relationship with you.'

Sandy was quite taken aback by Shaun's response, no one had ever said that to her before, yet although she was intrigued, she wondered if he was avoiding her question.

'You make a very valid point, Shaun, but it does matter because emotions or feelings can still run high for the ex. Time is supposed to be the healer. Without the healing, it can be hard for the person to engage healthily in a new relationship.'

Shaun smiled. 'Yes, I can understand where you're coming from. To answer your question, I've been single for about three months. It was an amicable split and I have no hang-ups. To be honest, Sandy, I don't really like discussing my past. I believe the past is the past. Although I do understand that a lot of people find it difficult to let go of the past, I just like to continue forward.'

'So, do you ever have any regrets or miss an ex-partner?' asked Sandy.

'Sandy, I'm not a robot, I do have feelings.'

'Sorry, Shaun,' interrupted Sandy, 'it's not that I think that you are a robot or anything like that. I just wondered if you don't have any hang-ups, or would you try again?'

'Here's your mango sorbet, enjoy,' said Michael, interrupting the conversation.

Sandy looked at Michael and smiled.

'I hope that this is as good as the last time I tasted it,' said Shaun with a big grin.

'Always good, in ten years it will still be good, Michael don't change recipe, that's why food always good.'

Shaun laughed as Michael walked back to the kitchen area.

'This is nice, it has a nice soft velvety texture, nice and sweet with a slightly tangy taste as it slides down your throat. Mm really nice!' exclaimed Sandy.

Shaun laughed. 'You sound like a food connoisseur. Yes, the food is nice, and I have wonderful company, I could not ask for a better date,' said Shaun.

Shaun reached across the table and held Sandy's hand. 'In answer to your question Sandy, which I have not forgotten, if I like the person, I will try not to lose her, and I would try to make the relationship work.'

Sandy smiled but she was not convinced about Shaun's answers; she felt that he was hiding something.

'So how long were you together before you both amicably ended the relationship?'

'We were together for five years, and after five years we ended the relationship and that happens sometimes. When it does, you leave the past behind and move forward like I am here doing with you, Sandy.'

Shaun was growing on her; she liked the way he responded to her questions.

'Well, the night is still young, Sandy,' said Shaun as he looked at his watch.

'What time is it?' asked Sandy.

'It's 10.30, we can go to a club if you like, or you can come back to my place. I live two streets away from Headcorn Road, and we can sit and talk more.'

'Your place? Wow, you're quick, how do I know that you won't try any hanky panky? It seems all too soon,' laughed Sandy. 'So, who do you live with?'

'No, I'm not thinking of any hanky panky, although I have not heard anyone say hanky panky in years, and in answer to your question, I live on my own. It's a two-bedroom converted house, only two floors and I live on the second floor. I have a boy and a girl. The girl is 17 and the boy is 19. I have two rooms for whenever they stay over.'

'I'm so sorry, I don't know why I did not ask if you had children, so what are their names?'

'It's okay, we're getting to know one another and I'm sure that at some point I would have mentioned them. The boy is Shaun Junior, and the girl is Donna.'

'Shaun Junior after his dad, I like that,' said Sandy smiling whilst sipping on her wine. 'So, do they spend weekends with you?'

Shaun smiled and sipped his wine. 'Not as much as I would like them to. They used to when they were younger but now, they're too busy. Now it's just dad can I have some money for this or that.' Shaun glanced at his watch again. 'Michael, can we have the bill please?'

Michael looked across at Shaun and raised his hand.

'So, what's the verdict Sandy, would you like to come back to mine?'

'Thank you for asking Shaun. Although it sounds very nice, I am a bit tired so I will decline your offer this time but please do ask again.'

Shaun laughed. 'I do like you, Sandy, I will definitely ask again in the near future.'

Shaun held out his hand for Sandy, she took the offer and held his hand. She smiled to herself as they walked back to the car.

'Would you like a different genre of music or artist?' Shaun asked as they sat in the car.

Sandy chuckled. 'What do you have Mr music maestro?'

Shaun smiled. 'Well, I have R&B, reggae, funky house, soul, rare groove.'

'I love your versatility, so do you have Lovers Rock?'

Shaun chuckled again. 'I know you think that you've got me, that's one genre of music that I may not have, but actually, my dear lady, I do have Lovers Rock.'

'Okay, okay, I'm just checking,' laughed Sandy. 'I'll have some Lovers Rock.'

'Lovers Rock, it is then,' said Shaun, smiling.

Sandy watched him fiddling around with his music player, then she heard 'Making Love' by Barry Boom. Sandy smiled

'Good enough for you, my dear?' asked Shaun as he looked at Sandy and smiled.

Sandy smiled back. 'Yes, good enough.' She relaxed back in the car enjoying the scenery.

'It's strange how you hardly notice anything when driving, it's nice to be a passenger for a change,' said Sandy, staring out of the car window.

'I agree with you, it's hard to really enjoy the journey because you have to focus on the road, especially here in London. There is so much traffic, but having wonderful company makes all the difference,' replied Shaun.

'I hope you don't mind me mentioning this, but I noticed that you looked at your watch a couple of times in the restaurant. I'm just wondering why?'

Shaun smiled. 'That's the counsellor in you - very observant. No particular reason, Sandy. I'm just time conscious. We had been there for a couple of hours and although Michael is nice, I am respectful of his establishment, plus I thought it would be nice to spend some more time talking with you outside of the restaurant.'

Sandy liked his reply; she studied his profile and noticed how relaxed he was.

'That's very thoughtful of you, I like the way you think. Has anyone ever told you that you look like Common?'

'Common the rapper/actor?' asked Shaun.

'Yes,' replied Sandy.

Shaun laughed. 'Yes, I've been told that by a few people, but I have a nicer complexion and I'm better looking.'

Sandy laughed. 'Yes, you do have a wonderful complexion although I don't know about the better-looking part.'

'I take it that you like Common?'

'He's alright,' replied Sandy with a big grin.

Shaun pulled up on Headcorn Road. He turned around and looked at Sandy. 'Well, here we are, my dear.' He took hold of her hand and stared into her eyes. 'You sure you don't want to come back to mine for a drink, I promise no hanky panky,' he laughed.

Sandy was very tempted, but she wanted to take her time and get to know him better.

'Thanks for the offer but I have to decline again my dear Common look-alike.' They both laughed.

'Then I hope to see you again soon.'

'That I can do,' replied Sandy

Shaun walked Sandy to her car. They looked at each other.

'Goodnight, my dear,' said Shaun.

'Goodnight and thank you for a lovely evening,' replied Sandy.

Shaun kissed her on the cheek and walked back to his car.

Chapter 11

Sandy awoke with a smile on her face. She looked at her clock it was only 8 a.m. She had no work scheduled for the day, so it was nice to relax in bed. Sandy went to the bathroom, then opened her curtains, and went back to bed. The sun brightened up her room and warmed her face, she closed her eyes and reminisced on her evening with Shaun. 'I like him,' she said to herself, 'maybe this is the one, maybe I found my husband.' Ping sounded her mobile, disturbing her thoughts; she grabbed her phone from her bedside table and giggled when she saw that it was a message from Shaun.

'Morning, my dear, I've been thinking of you all night, missed having your company for the rest of the evening. I am a patient man and long to see you again soon. Wanting to hear your voice, call me when you're awake'.

Sandy giggled and felt excited at the thought of Shaun lying in bed thinking about her which made her horny, her pussy began to throb. 'I could fuck him right now,' she said to herself. She pulled her knickers to one side and pushed her finger into her vagina stroking back and forth. Sandy moaned as she imagined his strong penis stroking her pussy in and out. Juice started to run out of her pussy, she stroked it more vigorously in and out until she gave a deep moan. 'I'm starving my fucking self of some good penis, I'll call him back later, maybe he'll get this pussy quicker than he thinks,' Sandy said to herself.

'Afternoon guys,' said Sandy as she entered the kitchen. 'What are you cooking?' she said whilst taking in the aroma.

'We've decided to cook today, mum, let you rest,' said Samuel, whilst pouring rice into the pot.

'Smells good guys, I'm sure that I can smell prawns.'

'You can, mum, no meat, we went shopping this morning and bought prawns and salmon and we're making season rice,' said Scott.

Sandy smiled. 'Season rice, that's one of my favourite dishes.'

Samuel and Scott smiled.

'Well, since you're both cooking, I'll catch up on some paperwork in my office.'

Sandy sat at her desk, looking out of her window into the garden. She smiled to herself as she sat back and thought about Shaun. She liked his dimples and his smile plus the fact that he had a resemblance to Common. 'I don't know why I did not notice that before,' she thought. 'Oh shit, I was supposed to call him back.' She quickly reached for her mobile phone; a sense of shyness and excitement came over her like a giggly teenager.

'Hi Shaun, sorry I took so long to call you, I awoke then fell back asleep again.'

'Afternoon, my dear lady, it's okay, just nice to hear your voice. Um, I just need to clear something up with you before we continue speaking.'

Sandy paused and raised her eyebrows.

'Okay,' she said.

'I did not invite you to my house last night to sleep with you. I just wanted to sit and chat to get to know you better, but I feel that I might have offended you.'

'No, Shaun, no offense taken,' interrupted Sandy chuckling to herself. 'I did not think that of you. I just knew that it would have not been wise for me to take you up on your offer, as we had been drinking.'

'Well, we would not want to blame anything on the drink,' laughed Shaun. 'So how did you like the date, and would you like us to meet up again?'

'I did enjoy the date, Shaun, and yes, I would like to meet up with you again,' replied Sandy with a big grin.

'Nice, that's what I like to hear, it's only fair that you choose the next place. I'm open to anything,' said Shaun.

'You're open to anything are you, well what if I said a nudist camp?'

'Now you're teasing me, Sandy, but I would not mind that at all. The chance to see what's beneath your clothes would be a pleasure. And I believe that I have quite a good physique.'

'Do you now?' replied Sandy with a smirk.

'Yes, I do, and you can see it anytime you're ready.'

Sandy laughed. This man was making her horny as hell.

'Well, on another note, I was thinking about dancing,' said Sandy.

'Dancing, that sounds good,' interrupted Shaun. 'There's a nice place called Silvarna, it's a nice little wine bar and they play great music.'

Sandy eyes opened wide, and she swallowed. She knew that there was a big chance of her seeing Ras or Teddy if she went there. She was not ready for that encounter, nor did she think that she ever would be.

'Silvarna, I've been there a couple of times. It is nice, but I was thinking of the Culture Club.'

'The Culture Club, where is that?'

'In North London, it's a nice place and the music is good.'

'What kind of music do they play?' asked Shaun.

'Mostly reggae like Dennis Brown, a bit of bashment sometimes. It's old skool so a mixture of everything.'

'Well, it sounds good. As long as I'm spending time with you, I don't mind. So, Friday or Saturday or the whole weekend,' laughed Shaun.

'It's Friday nights, so I guess I'll see you on Friday then. It's best to leave around 10 p.m. as it takes about an hour to get there.'

'That's okay, would you like me to pick you up this time?'

Sandy paused for a second. 'Um, yes, why not, that would be nice.'

'Text me your address, I'll be happy to be your chauffeur for the night.' Sandy laughed. 'Thank you, Shaun, that's very nice of you.'

'No problem, although I was thinking that it would be nice to see you sooner as Friday is nearly a week away and I would like to see that beautiful smile of yours. We could just go for a drink somewhere local, or you can come to my house. We can talk and relax, and I promise no hanky panky,' Shaun chuckled.

Sandy thought about it; Friday was some time away and she also wanted to see Shaun.

'Wednesday would be good,' said Shaun.

'Wednesday is also good for me; I will come by you. It will be nice to see your home. 7 p.m. if that's okay with you?'

'7 is good, it gives me enough time to get home from work and sort out things. I'll text you, my address. Looking forward to seeing you Wednesday, Sandy, and I promise I won't bite.'

'Then you'd better eat first before I come,' laughed Sandy.

Sandy smiled to herself as she hung up. 'I don't know what I get myself into sometimes,' she said to herself.

Sandy relaxed back in her chair with her legs up on her desk, reflecting on the situation with Ras and Teddy. 'I should have never entertained Teddy in the first place, everything about him was unstable, I don't know what I was thinking. I caused myself so much bloody drama for no reason,' she said to herself. She continued in thought, 'I miss Ras, although I don't know if I miss him or his penis. I do hope Shaun can fuck, otherwise I'll have to befriend Ras again.' Sandy chuckled to herself. Her thoughts were disturbed by her phone, she was happy to see Caroline's name.

'Hi girl, how's tings?' said Sandy in a chirpy voice.

'How's tings, I have not heard from you. I know it must be some man tickling your fancy which is why you've been so silent.'

Sandy laughed. 'It does need some deep tickling, but no one has tickled it as yet.'

They both laughed, Sandy knew that Caroline was a good friend and had her best interests at heart.

'Well, we need to catch up, I have something to tell you and Joan, so let's meet up at Cocoabana tomorrow evening at 8.30,' said Caroline.

'Why so late, babe?' Sandy asked

'I'm working a bit later than usual; I have to finish off some paperwork for a client.'

'Have you spoken to Joan yet?' asked Sandy.

'Just called her before I called you, she's cool with the time,' Caroline responded.

'Okay then, babes, tomorrow.' Sandy was curious about what Caroline had to tell them, she hoped that everything was okay.

Sandy was in deep thought as she drove to the wine bar. She remembered that the last time she went to Cocoabana was with Teddy. 'I don't know why I did not tell him that I wanted nothing to do with him when he told me about being in prison, I do put myself in some of the craziest situations sometimes.' As she pulled up, she saw Joan's car; she was surprised that Joan had arrived before her and Caroline as she was usually the last to arrive.

'Hi ladies,' said Sandy as she walked up to Joan and Caroline sitting in one of the corner seats. 'I did not see your car, Caroline, but I was surprised to see your car, Joan.'

'It's true, I know I'm always late, so you have to blame Caroline for me getting here early,' replied Joan.

'Yes, that right, blame me, I asked her to pick me up, and of course, because she's excited about what I have to say, she came early!' exclaimed Caroline.

'So now we know the secret of what to do to get Joan anywhere early, think up some mix-up and drama,' chuckled Sandy.

'We already have a tab so you can just order your drink,' said Joan to Sandy as the waitress approached their table.

'I'll have a Tropical Sunset, please,' said Sandy. Caroline and Joan both nodded in agreement. 'Better make that three then,' added Sandy.

Caroline placed both hands on the table and tapped her fingers.

'Oh my God!' screamed Sandy 'Is it what I think it is?'

Caroline grinned from ear to ear.

'No fucking way! You actually got him to propose?' asked Sandy.

Caroline nodded her head in response, holding up her finger to show the ring.

'What did you have to do, suck his dick for a week?' asked Joan.

'Fuck you, Joan, Lord forgive me, no I did not.'

'You know, I noticed the ring when we were in the car, but I did not pay any mind to it. It's a nice ring, Caroline, I'm happy for you. We should be ordering a bottle of champagne instead of cocktails to celebrate,' said Joan.

'What do you mean it's a nice ring, it's made by Vishi! It's a beautiful diamond band ring and damn expensive!' exclaimed Sandy.

'How do you know it's a Vishi ring?' asked Joan.

'Because I look at expensive rings. I don't want any cheap ring.'

'Well, you better stop talking to them broke arse men you keep meeting because they can't afford any expensive Vishi ring!' responded Joan.

Sandy rolled her eyes at Joan and turned to Caroline.

'So, Caroline, tell me what happened. I'm so excited,' said Sandy with a big grin on her face.

'To be honest, I'd had enough. I told him that we've been together for ten years and if he did not think that, by now, I deserved a ring on my finger then I'm gone. I told him to go, and I stopped answering his calls. After a week of ignoring him. he turned up at my door with a ring. He went down on one knee and proposed to me. The truth is if I had known what I know now I would have done this years ago.'

'Well, I'm happy for you and Patrick, at least you're halfway there, you just need to set the wedding date now,' said Sandy.

'That might be in another ten years,' laughed Caroline.

'Now you have the ring, go ahead and set the date. You take charge now, Caroline!' exclaimed Joan 'As for myself, I'm not sure about the married ting. I do love him. I mean we've been together for three years now and he's great with the children and especially great in bed. Things are good with us. I hear stories about people being together, they get married then they divorce. They say if it's not broken don't try to fix it. So, I think it's best to leave things the way they are.'

'I hear you, Joan, but I think that the reason why a lot of marriages break up is that for some reason people have an expectation which they did not have before the marriage,' said Sandy.

'I do not agree, Sandy, I think that the expectation should change because marriage is a deeper commitment,' said Joan.

'That's the problem though, Joan, you just said that if it's not broken don't try to fix it, so why change? That means you're trying to change what does not need fixing,' Sandy responded.

'You both have a point,' Caroline interrupted. 'I have had a relationship with Patrick for ten years. We have never lived together but we have spent a lot of time with one another. Things will change between us.'

'Okay, Caroline, but that is different because you have never lived with him. I'm talking about people who live together like Joan and her man. If you're both already happy with the way things are, then why change just because you're married? What more would you expect from him, Joan?' asked Sandy.

Joan took a sip of her drink and shuffled in her seat, then looked at Sandy.

'I supposed you're right, Sandy. I mean, he has always worked hard and looked after me and the children. I need nothing. I think, though, that if the shoe were on the other foot, he would want me to cook more or do more household chores, but I do get your point.'

'I wonder what Patrick is going to expect from me. I suppose I will have to put a lot more thought into cooking. I'm used to cooking whatever I want, the children are not fussy. Only on the weekends, I make the effort,' said Caroline.

'Speaking about the children, Caroline, have you told them about the engagement?' asked Sandy.

'Tell them,' laughed Caroline as she continued. 'They were right there when he proposed.'

Sandy and Joan looked at each other in astonishment.

'For real!' exclaimed Joan.

'Yes, Joan for real.'

'What did they say?' Sandy asked.

'Well, apparently he spoke to them beforehand and asked their permission. I was the only one in the dark. So, just like magic, they appeared when he was proposing.'

'He's damn lucky that you did not turn him down, that would have been a surprise,' said Joan.

'Oh, Joan,' laughed Sandy 'That was respectful of him to consider the children Caroline, I like that.'

'Yeh, it was. He is sweet, I suppose,' responded Caroline.

'Okay, Caroline, you can come back to earth now,' said Joan, snapping her fingers in front of Caroline. They all laughed.

'Anyway, enough about me now, what's new with the both of you?' Caroline asked.

'Well same man, same fuck,' responded Joan. 'We're going on holiday to Disneyland in Florida. I think I told you that last time. Well, he finally bought the tickets and booked the hotel.'

'That's nice, Joan, he is a very nice man, I'm happy for you,' said Sandy.

'Yeh, I'm looking forward to it,' replied Joan.

'Well, I've met someone. I just thought that I'd put that out there,' said Sandy with a smirk on her face.

'Every time we meet you've met someone,' responded Joan.

'Wow, Joan, you seem in some depressing mood this evening, at least she's moved on from those fools,' said Caroline.

'I agree,' said Sandy, 'You're just not your usual rude, cheerful, bubbly self.'

'I don't know, girls. I think that I'm just bored with life. I need something new and exciting. Even though you may do some foolishness, Sandy, at least your life is adventurous and exciting.'

'My life is full of drama, Joan, and indecisiveness, maybe you need to spruce up your love life,' Sandy responded.

'Girl, I have all different vibrators which my Marcus does not mind using. He's fantastic at eating my pussy too. Maybe I need some new dick,' laughed Joan.

'Or maybe, just do little feel ups outside the home or go to a hotel sometimes,' said Caroline.

'You know, you're right, Caroline. I like that idea, even a little feel up in the car sometimes. You know, do some spontaneous things. So, tell me about this new man Sandy, have you fucked him yet?'

'No Joan, I have not fucked him yet.'

'For real, that's a first!' Joan responded.

Caroline looked at Joan and laughed.

'Fuck the both of you. I'm not that bad, although I must admit I do want to fuck him.'

'So, why have you not fucked him yet?' Joan asked.

'Forget the fucking him part, who is this man and how or where did you meet him and why is it only now that I'm hearing about him, Sandy? You always run things by me, so how come you have not this time?' asked Caroline.

'I met him some time ago in Café Nero after my last supervision. At the time, I was going through all the stuff with Ras and Teddy, so I did not even think about him. It's weird though, because I had his number and I only called and spoke to him just before Ras and Teddy turned up at my door. The same day. Maybe new beginnings and endings all in one.'

'Awww, no fucking way!' shrieked Joan. 'You kept that fucking one quiet. Sorry Lord,' said Joan clearing her throat. 'You nearly make me choke on my drink.'

'Sandy, you went through so much and said nothing to me,' said Caroline.

'Look, Caroline, although you think that you are Sandy's big sister you are not so let go of the sentiment, plus I want to hear this juicy story.'

'I prefer to forget about it but anyway, it was my fault. I should have just told them that it was over rather than ignore their calls,' said Sandy with a grimace look.

'Well, I know what Michael is like, damn ignorant, so did they fight?' asked Joan with a big grin.

Sandy took a deep sighed. 'Nearly, if it were not for Scott and Samuel they would have.'

'Oh, my dear Sandy, lucky you've got those big strong men of yours. You must have been so embarrassed,' said Caroline, putting her hand on Sandy's arm.

'Yes, Caroline I was, it was so horrible, then to top it all off Teddy called me the next day and cussed me out. He made me feel so bad.' Sandy hung her head and stared into her drink.

'Hush,' said Joan, rubbing Sandy's shoulder. 'You see what I'm saying though. Sandy's life makes my life seem so damn boring. Nothing but pure excitement in this woman's life.'

They all laughed.

'It's not that exciting when you're going through it!' exclaimed Sandy.

'I know, Sandy, but your life is just full of so much drama,' laughed Joan.

'What I want to know is why that Teddy thinks that he has the right to cuss you out. He's a piece of shit, Ras should have punched him in the face!' exclaimed Caroline.

'No, Ras should not have, Caroline, and I'm glad that they did not fight,' responded Sandy.

'Well, I'm sorry that you had to go through all that, babe, good luck to bad rubbish. Now tell me about this new guy,' demanded Caroline.

'Thanks, Caroline. Well,' smiled Sandy, 'he has his own business and he's as handsome as hell. He and his dad have a business together, I should say. We met up last week Saturday and he took me out to dinner.'

'You finally meet somebody who has money, thank God,' interrupted Joan.

'Amen to that,' laughed Caroline.

'I swear that you two are taking the fucking piss! I don't know if I even want to continue.'

'Sorry, sorry,' said Joan and Caroline whilst still laughing. Sandy looked at both women and ordered another round of drinks before continuing.

'Like I was saying, he took me to a Thai restaurant in West London. It was nice.'

'So, when you say that he took you, that means he drove?' asked Caroline.

'Yes, he drove, Caroline,' responded Sandy.

'I like this man already,' responded Caroline, whilst taking a sip of her drink.

'What's his name?' Joan asked.

'Shaun, and he's got the most gorgeous dimples. He's dark and handsome, his body is fit, plus he resembles Common.'

'No, fucking way, he looks like Common? I know how much you like that man, you must be overjoyed,' said Joan with a big grin.

'Yes, well it is a bonus and I'm so fucking horny for him. But I'm just trying to keep it cool, although he keeps inviting me round to his house. He wants to see me before the weekend so I may see him Wednesday.'

'I've never known anyone who loves to fuck like you, Sandy,' said Caroline, shaking her head.

'That's only because she does not have a regular man. She fucks every so often, nothing regular, if she had a regular man, she would not fuck so much,' commented Joan.

'You may be right, Joan, when I was with Johnathon, my children's dad, we only had sex about once a week if that. Maybe that's why I'm making up for it now,' Sandy laughed.

'Now you know how I feel. I need to spice up my love life because I love to fuck also. Maybe I will go out for a drive with no knickers on and let John finger me whilst driving.' Caroline and Sandy laughed. Sandy was never surprised about the things that Joan said, she was as raw as they came.

'Life is too short, girl, you like the man, and you want to fuck him then do so. He's more worth fucking than the other two. If a man is going to fuck you and walk, he will do so whether he waits one week or one month. The man sticks around if he likes you and that is that. We're too mature to think about a waiting game, leave that to the young people,' said Joan.

'I agree with you, Joan, but just remember that you have a good man who adores you and the kids so just marry the man,' said Caroline.

'I may just do that,' responded Joan.

Chapter 12

Sandy pulled up outside Shaun's house. She felt nervous. She had brought a bottle of Cabernet Sauvignon with her. 'This is new,' she said to herself as she walked up to his door, she had never been to Michael's or Teddy's house. She was happy for the change, his rather than hers. She felt nervous and excited. Sandy noticed how clean his house was outside as she walked up to his white front door and pressed the bell.

'Hi, who is it?'

Sandy recognised his voice from the intercom and immediately felt butterflies in her stomach.

'Hi, it's your friendly Avon lady.'

'Well, I do hope that you have some nice goodies for me, come on up Avon lady.'

Sandy laughed to herself as she walked up the stairs to the front door. Shaun greeted her with a big smile. He was wearing navy blue shorts, no top, and a white towel around his neck.

'Lovely to see you,' Shaun said as he embraced Sandy. 'Welcome to my humble abode. So, what goodies does my friendly Avon lady have for me?'

'Just a bottle of red wine. I do hope you like it,' replied Sandy with a smile.

'I'm sure I will, although you did not have to buy anything. I already bought us a couple of wines plus I've cooked, nothing too big but I just thought in case you get hungry.'

Sandy smiled. 'That's nice of you, Shaun'. Sandy took off her shoes before entering Shaun's living room, as Shaun guided her to sit down.

'Make yourself comfortable whilst I put on a top. I've just had a shower so sorry for the lack of clothing.'

'Whatever, you just wanted to show off your chest,' Sandy bantered.

'Maybe I did,' replied Shaun with a big smirk on his face, as he walked off to get changed. Sandy fanned herself as she sat down, 'He's hot as hell,' she said to herself with a big grin. 'I could jump that body right now'. His pecs stood strong with his near six-pack and his body was dark and smooth. 'My pussy is pulsating, shit, calm down

Sandy, fuck I haven't had sex for ages. Okay, compose yourself, woman.'

Sandy looked around, admiring his grey deep-piled soft carpet. She liked that he only had a small part of wooden flooring near his front door then carpet all the way through. His house was painted light grey and white. Everything was very neat and in its place. His three-seater grey sofa was soft leather with matching armchairs at either side. The sofas were in the middle of the room. Behind the sofa against the wall was a music system and at the wall in front of the sofa was a 50-inch TV. In either corner of the room, he had a three-tier glass stand where he had placed pictures of his children and family. It was simplistic, with no clutter, and felt warm and cosy. She liked the neatness and simplicity of the room. Shaun walked in wearing a white vest with his navy -blue shorts.

'I did not leave you for too long, I hope?'

'No, I've just been admiring your décor and room, I like it.'

'Would you like a tour? It's small but I like it,' said Shaun.

'It looks like it's just the right size for you.'

Opposite the lounge was a door.

'That's my bedroom but it's best we start at the top and work our way back,' said Shaun whilst walking straight up the hallway. 'This is the kitchen as you can see.'

'It's a nice size of kitchen, quite spacious,' said Sandy.

'Yes, that's because everything is built-in, it makes the kitchen look a lot wider.'

Shaun's kitchen was black and white. The walls were white, and the appliances were black and silver. The cupboards and tabletops were black with silver specks. His fridge and freezer were behind a cupboard door. In the corner was a small, seated breakfast area.

'It's very nice, did you design it?' asked Sandy.

'Yes, I did, I took my time and worked on each room.'

'I'm impressed,' she said.

She nodded her head in approval. Shaun grew on Sandy even more. She liked what she saw, and she knew that he was more than a potential husband. Her children would approve of him plus he was much more suited to her than Ras or Teddy.

'Now walking back down the hall, this is the toilet with a small sink, and next door is the bathroom.'

The bathroom had both a bath and a shower cubicle with white and grey tiles on the wall and nice large white tiles on the floor, complemented with a large grey mat. Shaun pointed to two different doors.

'This is my children's room, it has two single beds, and this is my bedroom, which you can see later if you would like to.' Sandy smiled.

'We'll see,' she replied.

Sandy felt hot and knew that she definitely wanted to see his bedroom later.

'Take a seat, babe, while I get us a drink. Is red wine okay, I also have Bailey's?' he said, as they returned to the living room.

'Red wine is good, thank you.'

'I'll just put some music on.'

Shaun picked up the control and Keith Sweat singing 'Nobody' started playing. Shaun looked at Sandy and smiled as he walked out of the living room. 'Shit,' Sandy said to herself 'this fucking man is going to make me cum before he even fucks me. With his fuck me music and his fuck me body and his fuck me home, I'm just fucking hooked.' Shaun walked back into the room with two glasses of red wine.

'Thank you,' said Sandy as he handed her the glass of wine.

He walked out of the room and came back in with a small side table.

'So, what did you cook?'

'Just a pasta bake, would you like some now?'

'Sounds nice. I do like pasta bake but I'll have some a little later. Thank you for taking the time to cook something.'

Shaun sat down next to Sandy and stared into her eyes. Sandy lowered her eyes then looked back at Shaun. He continued to stare at her then bit his bottom lip. He took her glass of wine out of her hand and placed it on the side table. Shaun leaned into Sandy and started kissing her and sucking her lips.

'Good thing I have my fuck me dress on,' Sandy said to herself. Sandy was wearing a black V-necked pencil dress, easy to slip off in a hot moment. Sandy loved the way he kissed, and she started to get wet, she knew what she wanted. Shaun then eased off her and looked into her eyes.

'I really like you, Sandy. If you want me to stop I will, but I just don't want to be with you for tonight. I want a relationship with you. I can't stop thinking of you but if you feel that I'm going to fast just say.'

Sandy had butterflies in her stomach, she felt nervous and excited. 'It's time to grow up, Sandy,' she said to herself.

'No, it's not too fast, I like you too,' Sandy replied.

She sat up and straddled him, then held his face with both hands and started kissing him. Shaun stood up with his hand's clasped over her bum cheeks and walked with her. She wrapped her legs around his waist and held onto his neck.

'I think it's time that you see my bedroom now,' Shaun said as he laid her on his bed. 'Let me undress you.'

Sandy stared into his eyes and said nothing, she left Shaun to take full control. He rubbed his hands up her legs and clutched onto her knickers and slowly pulled them down. Sandy lifted her bum to help as he eased them off her legs and dropped them on the floor. She closed her eyes and took a deep breath. He sat her up and held her in his strong arms and unzipped her dress, she lay back whist he pulled her dress off.

'Open your eyes and look at me, Sandy,' commanded Shaun. She opened her eyes. 'I really like you, Sandy.' He held her face and kissed her deeply. His blanket felt soft beneath her body. Shaun clasped her breast and squeezed her nipple, then sucked hard on her breasts. Sandy groaned and reached for his penis, she stroked it back and forth. It felt big, thick, and strong, bigger than Teddy but a little smaller than Ras, which she liked.

'Have you got condoms?' whispered Sandy.

'Always, babes.'

Sandy smiled to herself, she liked that he was responsible, which made her even more relaxed to have sex with him. He started kissing her body and inner thigh. He pushed his finger inside her vagina, she bucked and yelped out.

'Shit, you're really wet,' said Shaun whilst stroking her vagina.

'Yes, I'm wet for you,' replied Sandy, breathing deeply.

Shaun grabbed the condom and put it on. He took his time pushing his penis into her vagina, teasing her bit by bit. Sandy held onto his neck and sucked on his lips. 'Relax babes, let me take my time.'

Shaun took his time stroking his penis back and forth in her vagina. He thrust deeper inside. Sandy groaned and held tightly to his blanket.

'Don't hold back, babes, I can feel that you want to come, relax and let it flow.'

Sandy screamed out and squirted over his blanket. Shaun shook and yelled whilst he came. Afterwards, he stared into her eyes and held her face.

'That was great, babes, I want you to be mine,' he said as he kissed her.

A sense of fear flowed through her body, she knew that this was real, and she liked him as well.

Sandy felt relaxed in his arms as he held her and kissed her.

'I've waited a long time to meet a woman like you, Sandy. I know that I promised no hanky panky but you're irresistible. I thought of making love to you from the first day I met you. I hope that this is as real for you as it is for me.'

Sandy blushed, her stomach churned, she felt tears come to her eyes, she then knew that she had been waiting for this for a long time.

'Yes, Shaun, this is as real for me as it is for you.'

Shaun held her face and stroked her cheek with his thumb.

'I promise that as long as you love me, I will love you and I will never hurt you.'

He kissed her deeply. Sandy felt his erect penis on her stomach, she opened her legs ready for round two.

As she drove home, Sandy could not stop thinking of all of the things Shaun had said to her. 'Shit, shit, shit, this is fucking real,' she said to herself as she pulled up in her driveway and relaxed back in her car. 'What are you afraid of

Sandy?' she asked herself as she rubbed her forehead. She thought back to her children's father whom she had loved very much, but the hurt she had suffered because of him was so devastating. It had taken her a long time to get over Johnathon; she had found it difficult to connect to men or trust them. Yet, she had loved Michael but had never let him know her feelings for him. She knew it was a waste of time. 'I'm so glad that I have supervision on Saturday. I need some help with putting all this into perspective although I know what Peter's going to say.'

Chapter 13

Hi Sandy, nice to see you, it's been a while.'

'Yes, Peter, it has been a while. I missed you last month, how was your holiday?' asked Sandy as they greeted each other with a handshake.

Peter motioned Sandy to take a seat.

'Well, it was not a holiday as my father became quite ill, so I had to fly back to Mauritius.'

'So, is he okay now?' Sandy asked, looking quite concerned.

'Yes, all is as well as can be expected, he is getting on in age. So, tell me what's been going on with you, Sandy?'

'It's been good, I've met someone new,' said Sandy, smiling.

'I do remember you mentioning that you had met someone new in our last meeting, so things are going well with this new man?'

'No, I'm not with that man anymore. I've let go of what is not good for me and met a man in a man's body.' Sandy smiled, feeling proud of her achievement.

Peter raised an eyebrow and peered at Sandy.

'Sounds good, we can address this after we speak about your clients.'

'Yes, of course, okay so the last meeting I spoke about client A. She is a 45-year-old black woman, who stayed with her younger partner because she feared being on her own.'

'I remember, we picked up on transference and you wanting to be the rescuing mother. Are you still seeing her?'

'No, we ended two weeks ago. I mention her because I thought about what you said during our session. I realised that she did not seek counselling because she wanted to end her relationship. She wanted to connect to her underlying issues as to why she continually attracts the same kind of men. When I'd let go of my anger, I was able to connect with her in a more empathetic way. In turn, this helped me to connect to myself. I was then able to do a lot of reflecting.'

'Sounds very good, Sandy, it's always key to remember that the client's issues are their issues. Although we empathise with their issues, they remain their issues. We are human beings so we will experience transference or sometimes project our issues/feelings onto clients. But it is very important to be aware, which is why supervision is vital. Our clients can often help us to become better therapists.'

'It's true, Peter, because client A helped me to release and forgive myself.'

Peter smiled and nodded his head in agreement. Sandy looked at her notes.

'My next client is client C, he is a 30-year-old accountant, white male. He is married and has a young son whom he says that he adores very much but he has fallen out of love with his wife. His son is two years old and he met his girlfriend about a year ago. He wants to leave his wife for this woman but is afraid that if he leaves her, she will make it very difficult for him to see his son. He feels stuck and he does not know what to do.'

'Apart from falling out of love with his wife, what are the other issues that he brings up?'

'He says that she has anger issues, and he finds it very difficult to communicate with her. '

'How long have he and his wife been married?'

'For about five years.'

'Have you discussed with him the relationship between himself and his wife before their son was born?'

'Yes, I have somewhat, he said that they used to travel a lot and have a lot of fun.'

'How many sessions have you had with this man?'

'Three,' replied Sandy, looking back at her notes.

'Do you feel that there may be some dynamics going on in the session between you? With him being a male and wanting to leave his wife with a young child?'

'I'm not sure. What I pick up on is his frustration. He wants me to see him as the victim and that he has no choice than to seek companionship elsewhere because of this crazy wife.'

'I think that you should address this within your session, to see how he feels about speaking to a female regarding his issue. He may also try to dominate the sessions. It's a good idea to address these issues for the therapy to begin. I also think that it would be beneficial to look at the relationship between him and his wife before having the baby. Moreover, to discuss when the change in his wife's behaviour began. It sounds like she could have suffered from post-natal depression when she had the baby. Which has not been recognised and therefore there has been a lack of understanding and support. Perhaps home became uncomfortable for him, and he found refuge in someone else and this, in turn, impacted on the home.'

'Yes, Peter, that makes a lot of sense,' said Sandy, taking notes. 'I feel that he just wants to rush the sessions in order to find an easy way out.'

'I don't entirely agree, Sandy. He seeks counselling for a reason, don't let him control the sessions. Explore the relationship between him and the wife. It is important to find out if she had support when she had the baby and to identify any change in her behaviour. He needs to recognise the change and see the situation through new eyes. I also feel that he should consider couple counselling.'

'Yes, I agree, thank you, Peter.'

'If you do not have any other clients to discuss, we have 40 minutes left to talk about this new relationship of yours,' said Peter.

Sandy smiled. 'No, that's it.' She placed her notes in her bag.

'Well, after I meet with you, I always go to Café Nero, to reflect on our sessions,' she began to explain.

'That's good,' interrupted Peter. 'I sometimes see your car when I'm leaving, and I was curious as to why you were still parked there. I may have joined you if I had known. Sorry for interrupting you, continue.' Peter smiled, he placed his notes on his desk and adjusted himself in his chair.

Sandy smiled at Peter's comment; although she liked his advice, she enjoyed spending time to herself reflecting.

'Well, on this particular occasion I met this new guy, his name is Shaun. He approached me whilst I was having my hot chocolate and muffin. He seemed charming enough and the conversation between us flowed nicely. When I was about to leave, he asked for my number. I took his instead because I was unsure if I wanted to hear from him although he was very charming.'

'So, you met him after our last supervision meeting?'

'Yes.'

'I do hope that I did not scare you off meeting men.'

'No, Peter,' Sandy chuckled, 'but you gave me food for thought. 'Plus, remember I said I had met someone new?'

'Yes, I remember, and you said that you were not sure about him.'

'Yes, he was someone that I had known for a long time, and he had always liked me. What I've learned is that some men should just stay on the side of liking. There is a reason why a relationship never ensued in the first place, and it should remain that way.'

Sandy took a deep breath and exhaled, she relaxed back in the chair, just the memory of Teddy exhausted her.

'Some men always want a piece of the pie, Sandy, and they will continually watch and make advances towards the pie until one day they get to taste the pie, then they are stuck. They don't know what to do because they never believed they would get to taste it in the first place. When you have a slice of pie, Sandy, you'll wonder if you should have it with custard, ice cream, cream, or on its own. Men become confused, they don't know what to do, they have no plan and a man without a plan is going nowhere so it's inevitable that it won't work.'

Sandy sighed. 'Yeh, a man without a plan, that's what it was.'

'So, tell me about this Shaun now.'

Sandy's face lit up. 'He's tall, dark and handsome and resembles Common.

'He has a construction company which he owns with his father. He also owns his home. On our first date, he took me to a Thai restaurant. He is so wonderful to talk to, I feel at peace and I'm happy. Plus, the sex is fantastic.'

Peter laughed. 'I know that the sex part is very important to you, Sandy, although I think that you use sex as a cover for wanting to be close to someone. So, what do your children and friends think of him so far?'

'My friends like that I'm happy but they have not met him yet. The children like him. I invited him round for dinner, they all liked him. He can contract work from my son who has his own telecommunications company. Cassandra said I had finally found a man in a man's body. She likes him, plus she says that he's good looking. Cammy's happy that there's no more Ras or Teddy. Sophia likes that he owns his home and I'm happy.'

'Sounds good, Sandy, I'm glad that you finally met a nice man who is on your level and that you can relate to, which is very important. How do you feel about Ras now? I know that you cared about him for a long time. Do you think that you have finally moved on emotionally from him?'

Sandy relaxed back in the chair and sighed. 'Shaun has helped me to move on and realise that I deserve better. In answer to your question, the way we ended was not so good. I have not told you what happened, but I wish that we had not parted the way we did. Still, I was honest with him, and I still do think about him sometimes, but I know that there is no going back and it's time to move on.'

'People sometimes think that to move on you have to stop loving the person but that's not the case. You just need to love yourself more and know your worth. It does not mean that you stop loving or caring about that person, it just means that it's time to walk away. It takes a lot of strength and willpower not to turn back. On that note. Sandy, our time is up. I'll book you in for the same time next month.'

'Thank you, Peter, see you next month.'

Sandy walked to Café Nero and ordered her hot chocolate and muffin. She found a nice corner and sat down, noting that the place was less busy than usual, probably due to the school summer holiday. She thought about the plan she, Joan, and Caroline had to marry in a year and concluded that it had gone quite well, as ludicrous as it had sounded in the beginning. Caroline had finally got her ring and would marry next year in June. Joan had finally accepted Marcus's proposal and would also marry sometime next year. Sandy was finally in a decent relationship and was sure that he was going to propose. She had learned that it was not all about the ring, it was about being settled in a loving caring relationship, moving on from the past and letting go of the hurt and pain and not being afraid to experience true love.

Sandy's thoughts were interrupted by her phone vibrating, it was a private number. She hated answering private numbers but was concerned that it might be a client. 'Afternoon,' said Sandy.

'Sandy, it's me Ras, I need to see you, we need to talk.'

Chapter 14

Sandy's heart pounded; she did not know if she should answer him or hang up the phone.

Sandy paused, then took a deep beath. 'Hi Michael, we have not spoken for a long time, how are you?'

Ras is Sandy's pet name for Michael. Calling him Michael indicated indirectly to Ras that she had emotionally detached from him.

'So, we're back to Michael now, Sandy, I know you've moved on, I've seen you with your man. I know who he is, I've seen him at Silvarna's.'

Sandy's heart skipped a beat, she wondered where Ras had seen them. The last thing she wanted was for Ras to know Shaun. Sandy had built her little kingdom around Shaun, and she wanted it to stay that way.

'So where did you see us?'

'Don't worry about that, Sandy, all I can say is that he's not what you think he is. Anyway, I did not call you to talk about him, I...'

'What do you mean that he's not what I think he is?' Sandy interrupted.

Sandy felt quite annoyed; she did not know if Ras really knew something or if he was just making up a story.

'I did not call you to speak about no next man, Sandy!'

'So, what did you call me for, Ras? We have not spoken for at least two months or more. Now you're calling me to tell me that the man that I am seeing is a liar!'

'Sandy, calm down! I did not tell you that anyone was a liar. I called you to talk about us and what has changed in my life.'

'What do you mean us? There is no us, Ras. I don't even know if there ever was an us.'

'Look Sandy!' shouted Ras, 'I did not call you to argue with you. It's you that fucked up, remember! I turned up at your door and see another man standing in your driveway. You did not even have the respect to call me and talk to me at any time. It's as if what we had meant nothing to you, as if I don't have feelings, Sandy.'

'I know, I'm sorry,' said Sandy.

She had a feeling of *dejà vu* but with Ras instead of Teddy. She had always felt guilty about the way things had ended with Ras. She knew that he was right with what he was saying.

'Then I see you with next man, it's as if the two years we had meant nothing to you, Sandy, you just moved on just like that.'

Sandy did not know what to say, she missed him, and she knew that she had handled the situation very badly. However, Sandy knew that if she had phoned him, their so-called relationship would start back up again. She wanted to move on. Sandy had enough of her children and friends calling him a broke arse. She wanted something new and different, and Shaun was new and different or so she thought. Sandy felt confused, her head and her heart were in two different places.

'Look, Sandy, I want to talk to you, that's all. Just come to my place. I have a little flat now, Sandy. Just come and see my place and let us talk even if it's only for 20 minutes. I deserve that at least, Sandy.'

'In two years, you have never invited me to your place. So, we had to break up for you to invite me?'

'Sandy, you don't understand, I had nowhere to invite you to. I was going through a lot, and I needed to sort myself out.'

'Okay, Ras text me your address, I'll come around at 6 this evening.'

'Thanks, Sandy, I'll text you the address now.'

'I need to know what he knows about Shaun,' Sandy said to herself. She was spending the night with Shaun, and he did not expect her until around 8 p.m. Sandy no longer wanted her hot chocolate and muffin; she did not know if going to see Ras was the right thing to do. 'I need someone to talk to, but I know that I can't talk to Caroline or Joan because they'll just cuss me out. I'll check Sophia, she's easier to talk to,' she said to herself.

'Hi, mum,' said Sophia, 'what a nice surprise.'

'Hi, honey,' said Sandy, giving Sophia a big hug. 'I just thought that I'd stop by and see you and the girls.'

'Sorry, mum, they're not here, Danny took them out for the day. So, what's wrong, mum? I can see that something is bothering you.'

'You know me well Sophia, guess who I got a phone call from today?'

'Teddy.'

'No not Teddy,' replied Sandy with a grimace look.

'Then it must be Ras.'

'Yes, he said that he had seen me and Shaun together and he knows him because he's seen him at Silvarna's a few times.'

'So, what if he knows him and he's seen you both together? You're not with him anymore. Does Shaun know him?'

'I don't know, I don't think so. Though all of these men seem to know each other one way or the other. He says that Shaun is not what I think he is.'

'He's just jealous mum, don't listen to him, what could he possibly know about Shaun?'

'I don't know. He also said that he has his flat now and he wants me to go round and see him.'

'You're not going to go around there, are you mum? it's just a ploy to get you back. You've finally met someone nice, don't let him spoil it for you.'

'I hear you, Sophia, but the truth is I've always felt bad about how we ended. Going to see him will make me feel better plus I do want to know what he knows about Shaun.'

'Mum, who cares what he knows about Shaun? Let him keep it to himself, just forget him, mum.'

Sandy could see that Sophia was becoming agitated, maybe talking to her had not been a good idea.

'You're right, Sophia, good thing I spoke to you first, I will just forget about it.'

'Mum don't try and outsmart me. If you go and see him, you're going to mess everything up with Shaun. Think about what you're doing before you do it.'

'You're right, I won't go. I'm spending the night with Shaun in any case. I'm going home now to cook and get myself ready.'

'Okay mum, take care and remember what I said.'

'Yes Sophia, goodbye,' replied Sandy.

Feeling exasperated as she got into her car, she looked at her phone and saw that Ras had sent his address. It was in Coulsdon, only a 20-minute drive away. Her phone rang. It was Shaun.

'Hi sweetie,' said Sandy with a big smile.

'Hi, my lovely lady, looking forward to seeing you later.'

'I'm looking forward to seeing you too, sweetie. I'm just going to stop and check in on Caroline on my way to you.'

'Okay, lovely, so when am I going to meet your friends?' asked Shaun.

'Soon, babes. I told you that I'm going to do a barbecue. I can introduce you to my friends and the rest of my family there.'

'Okay, lovely lady, I'll see you soon, and wear something sexy.'

'That's just standard, sweetie, bye.'

Sandy liked Shaun; they had grown much closer over the past couple of months. He had not displayed any behaviour which made her feel that she could not trust him. Yes, there were missed calls here and there and the odd weekend that he had to work to finish a project. That's normal, it happens sometimes. He always called her back before the end of the day, unlike Ras or Teddy. She still needed to know why Ras had made that statement. It was also a good opportunity to get the ending with him that she had always wanted so she could stop feeling so guilty. Although she could not understand why she felt guilty because he was so full of shit, yet her conscience said otherwise.

Sandy reached home and decided to cook baked chicken with rice. She also seasoned a leg of lamb for Sunday. Nice and easy, she thought to herself, not too long in the kitchen. She knew that once the dinner was sorted for her adults, she could easily find something for herself.

Sandy started to get ready for her night with Shaun. She thought about what she was going to wear. Keeping in mind that she was going to see Ras, she did not want Ras to feel that she was looking sexy for him. Sandy decided to wear her red lace bra with matching crotch-less knickers. She packed her sheer open front black kimono to wear over her bra and knickers to add a bit of seduction. Although Shaun did not need any seducing, she chuckled at the thought. Over her underwear, she wore a tight-fitting short black dress which stopped at her thighs and open-toed black wedge sandals. To complement the outfit, she wore diamante stud earrings with a matching necklace. While she was standing in the mirror attaching her chain around her neck, Cammy and Cassandra entered her room.

'You look nice, mum, where you off too?' asked Cassandra.

'Thanks, Cass, I'm spending the evening with Shaun.'

'Um, um, you sure you're going to see Shaun?' asked Cammy.

Sandy turned around and looked at her daughters who both stood still, staring at her.

'What's wrong with the both of you? Why are you both looking at me like that and questioning me about Shaun?' asked Sandy with a curious look, hoping Sophia had not said anything to them.

'Getting straight to the point, mum, we spoke to Sophia, and she wanted us to make sure that you were not going to see that broke arse idiot Ras,' said Cammy.

'But I told them, mum, that you're not so stupid and you would not mess up what you have for that fool. You know if you go and see him, he will mess everything up for you,' said Cass.

Both of her daughters continued to stare at her, waiting for an answer. Sandy was shocked and annoyed.

'Look at you both stepping into my room like a twin gang questioning me as if I'm a child or have committed a crime. Sophia should not have said anything to you. It was just an idea I was running by her, and I told her the reason why.'

'So, you're not going to see him then, mum?' asked Cammy with a serious look.

'I already told you both that I'm not going to see him, so leave me alone and don't ask me any more questions.'

'Okay, mum, you look nice, enjoy,' said Cammy.

'I told them, mum, I have more faith in you than they do,' said Cassandra.

'Goodbye,' said Sandy, staring at them both.

Sandy sat down on her bed, she felt upset and betrayed by Sophia, 'Fuck,' she said to herself. 'I know that they want the best for me, but they just don't understand, I have to do what I have to do. I'm in control of myself, nothing can happen with Ras if I don't want it to happen. And I definitely don't want it to.'

Sandy knew deep down that she was lying to herself, she missed him, and she wanted to feel his touch just for one last time. She looked at her phone and realised that it was 5.45 p.m. She grabbed her bag and left.

Sandy parked outside Ras's flat; she took a deep breath. 'You're in control, Sandy, nothing can happen unless you want it to happen and nothing is going to happen,' she repeated to herself like a mantra. She rang his doorbell, she heard nothing, she rang it again, still nothing. She felt frustrated and hoped that she had not come all this way for no reason. She took her phone out of her bag and rang him.

'Hi Ras, where are you? I'm ringing your doorbell.'

'Oh, sorry, the bell does not work properly, I'm on my way down to let you in.'

Ras opened the front door, she looked at him and smiled. He had on a white T-shirt and white shorts with the Nike sign on both garments.

'I'm happy you came. Sandy, I'm on the top floor.'

The passage was unkempt, papers and letters lay on the dirty old carpet; the whole passage had an old damp smell. Ras lived two flights up.

'How long have you lived here?' asked Sandy.

'A month now, this is only temporary until I get something else. The people downstairs are too messy and nasty, they don't keep down here clean.'

'Yes, I can tell,' said Sandy, screwing up her face.

'I know it's not like your posh house, Sandy, but at least it's a start. Anyway, let me show you around.'

Sandy could see that Ras had recently moved in as the flat had little furniture.

'It's only small, but it's good enough for me. This is my kitchen, there was already a cooker and small fridge left here when I moved in, so I just cleaned them up. They look as good as new.'

'Yes, it does look clean,' said Sandy. She could see from the way Ras was looking at her that he wanted her approval. Ras smiled and walked towards the bathroom.

'You can see that I brought new mats and shower curtain, everything is nice and clean. This is my bedroom and before you say anything, Sandy, yes the bed is new, and the sheets are clean.'

'Why do you have to say it like that, I have not said anything,' chuckled Sandy.

'Um, I know you, Sandy, come here and stop acting like we are strangers.' Ras pulled her into his arms and started kissing her.

'Stop,' said Sandy, trying to pull away from him. 'I did not come here for this; I just came to see how you are.'

Ras continued to hold Sandy tight around her waist and stared at her. That intense look always went straight to her vagina. 'You're in control. Sandy,' she said herself. But Sandy knew that she was struggling in vain, so she just relaxed and stared back at him.

'I miss you, Sandy, I really missed you. I know that I continuously fuck up and your children do not like me. Sandy, I love you and I know that you love me too otherwise you would not have come.'

Sandy was speechless. Ras had never told her that he loved her, nor had she told him. Yet it was unspoken feelings that they both felt.

'Maybe you should have told me how you felt and treated me a lot better when we were together, it's too late now, I am in a relationship,' said Sandy releasing herself from his grip.

'You're mine, Sandy, you've always been mine, no next man can fuck you as I do.'

Sandy knew he was right; her pussy had become wet just on hearing his words. She knew her children would be upset with her but what no-one knows won't hurt them.

Sandy sat down on the bed; she took off her shoes so that she could relax. Ras smiled and sat beside her.

'I've got an hour before I have to be where I have to be, so let's talk. I think that I owe you that much,' said Sandy.

'There's nothing to talk about, this pussy is mine,' said Ras as he rubbed his hands up and down her legs.

Sandy laughed. She looked at him and put her hand on his cheek and kissed him. Ras laid her down on the bed and started kissing her passionately. She held the back of his head and kissed him deeply. She missed him and wanted one last fuck. She knew that despite him telling her that he loved her, she could not be in a relationship with him. Ras rubbed his hands between her thighs, she opened her legs for him.

'Take off your knickers,' he commanded.

'I don't need to, they're crotch-less.'

Ras smiled. 'Yes, easy access I like that.' He pushed his finger into her vagina and rubbed it back and forth with the juices from her vagina. He continued to push his finger into her vagina and back out again, rubbing her clitoris and in and out again. Sandy opened her legs further and gave a deep moan.

'You can make as much noise as you want, there is no-one here, just us as it should have been from long time. You're so fucking wet, this pussy is mine,' said Ras, staring intensely at Sandy.

'Aww, this feels so fucking good. I've needed this for so long,' said Sandy, breathing deeply. She held his face and kissed him deeply, sucking his tongue and lips.

'You're so wet I don't think that I need to use any lube.'

'It's okay, babes, just put the condom on. I need to feel your penis inside of me.'

Ras grabbed the condom from the table near his bed and put in on. Sandy knew that she would not tear because she was getting regular sex from Shaun, and he was only a little smaller than Ras.

'Aww fuck,' groaned Ras, 'this pussy feels so good,' he said as his penis stroked back and forth inside her.

Sandy held onto his locks and screamed out 'Oh yes, this fuck feels so fucking good, no-one can fuck me like you babes, no-one!'

They both shook and came together, Ras staring into her eyes as he kissed her.

'Forget where you have to go, stay the night with me,' he said.

'No, I can't, I have to go. I need to use your bathroom; can you give me a clean towel please?'

Sandy went into the bathroom and freshened up, 'Fuck, Sandy, you give yourself so many problems due to sex, but the fuck was proper,' she said to herself. Sandy still loved Ras, but she knew that it would be silly to leave Shaun for him. Although it seemed that Ras was getting his life together, she knew that she could not take that risk, plus the children would crucify her. She walked back into the bedroom, sat on the bed, and put her sandals on.

'Why can't you just call Caroline and tell her that you will see her tomorrow or another day and spend the night with me? We have not seen each other for a long time, Sandy.'

'I'm not going to see Caroline, Ras.'

'So, where are you going then?' asked Ras staring intensely at her.

'I'm going to see Shaun.'

'So, you just fuck me then go and see your man?'

Sandy could see the lines forming on his forehead and his eyes becoming red, she knew he was upset with her.

'Look Ras, I stopped by to talk to you, and you turned me on. I don't understand why you're upset, he's my man, not you.'

'Fuck you, Sandy!' shouted Ras.

Sandy stood up and walked to the front door. Ras followed her.

'So that's it then, Sandy. You're fucking cold, you don't give a fuck about me.'

'I cannot give you what you want, Ras, it will not work. It does not matter how I feel about you or you feel about me, it just won't work. You had two years Ras, two years and you fucked around and took us for a joke. I cannot and will not go back. Fucking you one last time was an ending for both of us,' said Sandy, with tears rolling down her cheeks.

'It was an ending for you, Sandy, not for me, just go to your married man!'

Sandy froze on the spot. 'What did you just say?'

'I said go to your fucking married, man, that's right Sandy, your man is married, and he is still with his fucking wife.'

To be continued….

Milton Keynes UK
Ingram Content Group UK Ltd.
UKHW051847280624
444890UK00036B/761

9 781908 552778